Endorsements for:
Forming The Leader's Soul:
An Invitation To Spiritual Direction

A quiet revolution has been taking place in the American church for several decades. It involves the recovery of the art of spiritual direction and a deepening of the contemplative life—prayer and discernment and friendship in a society and church that has become increasingly superficial and depersonalized. My sense is that it might well be the most significant work being done in the church today. Morris Dirks provides a most attractive and comprehensive invitation to both pastors and laity to participate.

Eugene H. Peterson
Professor Emeritus of Spiritual Theology
Regent College, Vancouver, BC

This is a book both generous and wise. Morris Dirks serves up a feast—a lively history of the ancient art of spiritual direction, a practical field guide for veterans and novices alike, a vivid portrait gallery of men and women transformed by this practice, and a step-by-step manual for engaging spiritual direction. And not a sentence drags. I have only a single complaint to lodge: Morris didn't write it sooner. A must-read for all leaders who long to go the distance and plumb the depths.

Mark Buchanan
Author of *Your Church Is Too Safe* and *Spiritual Rhythm*

Learning to hear God in the whimsical play of our grandchildren or in the intensity of a harsh conflict requires a turning toward a voice, a presence that invites us to be formed into a greater likeness of Jesus.

Morris Dirks offers a rich feast of honesty, wisdom, and practice to draw our senses and heart to the wonder of this foundational journey. Morris is a man of deep integrity, who knows his own brokenness and false attachments, and he has heard the call of life and love in the sinews of his heart. This book will be richly used as a sturdy and life-giving guide to taste and see the goodness of God.

Dan B. Allender, PhD
Founding President, Seattle School of Theology and Psychology
Professor of Counseling Psychology

For the majority of evangelicals, spiritual direction is a lost art. We are long on discipleship, accountability relationships, mentoring, coaching, and counseling. In fact when someone brings up the subject of spiritual direction, it is not uncommon to mistake it for one of these other valuable practices. Morris Dirks' *Forming The Leader's Soul* is quite possibly the most important book you will read on the subject of self-care. Morris transparently discloses some of the deep struggles and pain he experienced along the way as a spiritual leader . . . and the transformative role that spiritual direction played in his recovery of healing and joy. It is not overstating the matter to say that if you put into practice what Morris describes in this book, you will be forever changed for the better!

Charles J. Conniry, Jr., PhD
Vice President and Dean
George Fox Evangelical Seminary/George Fox University

Looking over the emotional edge, fearing one may fall over then fearing you might not, is what Morris has described in frightening detail. We think his moment of the "deep dark night of the soul" is uncommon and unusual among those in public ministry. Not so. His recounting of feeling lost, and at best unsure, sounds familiar. What is not so familiar is his solution: spiritual friendship. Yet, it is obvious, once he tells us, and logical once he describes it. From the anguish of personal life, Morris Dirks, in *Forming The Leader's Soul: An Invitation to Spiritual Direction*, helps those in public leadership into a rich and full understanding of their needs of self, the reoccurring demands of the call and various ways of rooting life in the soil of replenishing nurture. Morris provides us with a "reader," a course 101, which is the place each of us will start in understanding how to avoid disabling soul-darkness. He lovingly and with good research opens us to the ways and provision of the Spirit as we engage in Kingdom life. This book read earlier in my calling would have kept me from wandering in desert places, helping me to find those springs and wells that renew the spirit. Read it; then pass it on to those who will in time yearn for deepness and those you see whose lives would be lifted by this clear and refreshing letter of hope.

Brian C. Stiller
Global Ambassador, World Evangelical Alliance
President Emeritus, Tyndale University College & Seminary

I've been a pastor and worked with pastors for nearly 30 years. You don't have to convince me that ministry is, in the words of one writer, a "hard calling." Leadership is lonely, but as Morris Dirks eloquently reminds us in *Forming The Leader's Soul*, we don't have to go it alone, nor should we. Leading others in ministry doesn't mean we have to shove aside our deepest need to know others and be known by others. In this clear and readable book, Dirks guides us expertly through the theology and practice of spiritual direction, a tradition that has guided and sustained leaders for generations but is strange and unfamiliar to many evangelicals. Shaped by Dirks' own journey of desperation and discovery, and loaded with practical, biblical wisdom, *Forming The Leader's Soul* is a rich and timely resource for all ministry leaders. Read it, then do it. For the sake of your soul.

Robb Redman, ThD
Dean and Associate Professor of Theology and Ministry
Multnomah Biblical Seminary

Forming The Leader's Soul:

An Invitation to Spiritual Direction

MORRIS DIRKS

For Ruth

My wife and lifelong soul friend

Contents

Introduction

If you are new to the world of spiritual direction, or have been on this journey for years, *welcome*. I am a ministry leader who discovered spiritual direction later in life. Even though this is an ancient practice, one that dates back to the early church, I was simply not aware of the need for spiritual guidance. However, I came to realize that spiritual direction was crucial if I was going to maintain vitality and continue in ministry with passion and emotional strength.

What precipitated this shift in my journey? The answer is *pain*. After over two decades of joy-filled engagement as a pastoral leader, I fell into a season of emotional despair and ministry confusion—a season that changed everything! I have often asked myself: *How did I fail to anticipate this crisis? Why was I so unprepared for the emotional train wreck that took place in my soul?* I now see that spiritual direction would have provided a place of protection and discernment amid the challenges of life and ministry. I have come to believe that every leader needs a spiritual guide.

I thank God for leading me into that unexpected "dark night." Out of the ashes of my disorientation, he has radically reshaped my way of life and birthed a vision for the spiritual and emotional health of other leaders. As the Founder and Director of SoulFormation, I am joined by a staff that believes spiritual direction is a critical pathway toward well-being in life and ministry.

I meet with ministry leaders every week. More often than not, I discover they are submerged in a world that is demanding, complicated, and emotionally draining. Many of them express feelings of being overwhelmed. They are looking for avenues of renewal. Spiritual direction presents a strong foothold toward sustainable ministry, yet most leaders forge ahead while remaining unaware of this time-tested opportunity for support.

This book is for leaders who feel that true spiritual formation is *relational* at its core. Such a conviction invites us to a serious investigation of spiritual direction. I care deeply about leaders and trust that the pages to follow will open a window that deepens your experience of God and strengthens your ministry foundation in him.

1

In Need of Spiritual Direction:
One Leader's Journey

My Journey into Spiritual Direction

"I have totally and completely lost my way." Those were the first words to come out of my mouth as I spoke to the psychiatrist in the opening moments of my initial appointment. Tears streamed down my cheeks. My wife, Ruth, sat beside me, a true *soul friend* who had walked with me through the past four years as I slowly, but surely, slid from optimism and joy in ministry into an extended season of painful disillusionment. I walked into the psychiatrist's office out of sheer desperation. I had already been to a Christian therapist, but the depression and anxiety remained lodged deep in my soul. Somehow, I had to find my way back to emotional and spiritual equilibrium. I never dreamed ministry disappointment would result in needing professional help as a necessary step to recovery! I was overwhelmed by shame.

Let's back up. Four years before this meltdown I was bidding farewell to a church family after serving there for seventeen years. This extended season in ministry had exceeded all my dreams. It was my first lead pastorate and, from start to finish, everything was mysteriously graced with joyful experiences. Together we celebrated an ongoing period of spiritual and numerical growth that few pastors ever have the privilege of knowing.

As we gathered to say good-bye to that congregation, tears streamed down my face—tears of sheer gratitude and joy. As Ruth and I looked across the hundreds of people who came to send us off, I felt like my role as a pastor was a perfect fit. These had been the best years of our lives and we ended them with a sense of wonder for all God had done in us and through us.

After the farewell experience came to an end, my mind shifted to the future. I anticipated much more to come; it was time to write the next chapter in the ministry journey of my life. What followed was a move to a new city, a new church, a new challenge, and the pursuit of a new dream. Optimism and expectancy were bursting in my soul! The church was perfectly located in the high-tech corridor of a major city. From what I could see, this was a community of people with strong leadership, significant resources, and an expanding vision. A whole new world was opening up.

Yet, shortly after we landed, I began to sense that my spirit was deeply unsettled. Within a few weeks I realized something significant was out of alignment at the heart of this community. I remember feeling unsafe at an emotional level. As the months and years went by, that uneasy feeling was never resolved. It only deepened.

I accepted the call to this church knowing there was a history of tension. Previous pastors had faced significant challenges. Yet, somehow the implications of their story didn't register when I accepted the call. I arrived with confidence and optimism, believing that my experience would be different. I fully believed that I was up to the task. Yet, in time I discovered things—things I didn't know about the church when I arrived. More importantly, I discovered something else that was very unsettling. There were unresolved issues in my own soul that I had not yet encountered—concerns that were about to surface through this long season of disillusionment. New levels of self-awareness were needed if God was going to shape the core of my identity around his dreams and not mine.

It took three years to hit rock bottom. My optimism gave way to suspicion, then pessimism, and finally a deep cynicism. Along the way I remember sitting in the medical doctor's office describing my stress-related symptoms and secretly wondering if he could take out his prescription pad and write something on it—something for the church board: *Your pastor needs a leave of absence due to stress. I recommend several months.*

I should tell you that while I was slipping into this emotional and spiritual crisis, the church was taking significant steps forward. On the scoreboard everything was heading in the right direction. The congregation had doubled in size, staff had been added, and new ministries were developing to reach the community. Yet, while this was happening, our leadership team seemed irretrievably stuck in an ongoing pattern of distrust and disappointment. As I attempted to bring everyone onto the same page, I found myself working harder and harder as my soul was sinking deeper and deeper into hopelessness. I kept soldiering on until that day when we landed in the psychiatrist's office. I had nothing left to give. Anxiety and depression ruled my soul. The words "I have totally and completely lost my way" were my final admission of defeat.

It wasn't any kind of moral indiscretion that brought me to this place. There were no hidden sins that had suddenly surfaced to shatter my integrity and ministry dreams. Rather, it was a slow, steady, and systematic erosion of my vision and self-confidence. The ministry had worn me out. I never expected it could. Not me! I was always the successful student, athlete, leader, and pastor. For more than twenty-five years I had thrived in various ministries, moving seamlessly from one challenge to the next. Yet, somehow, I had derailed.

Richard Rohr, a well-known Franciscan friar and priest offers these words for people who find themselves in a season of disorientation: "If you are lucky, God will lead you to a situation you cannot control, you cannot fix, or you cannot even understand. At that point true spirituality begins. Up to that point is all just preparation."[1] I was at that point! God was unearthing the twisted strategy by which I had desperately tried to maintain control, a strategy that I was not even aware of until I reached that place where *the situation could not be controlled, fixed, or even understood.*

When I finally hit that wall, my spiritual and emotional recovery plan included something more than doctors and counselors. Over the years I learned of another source of guidance and wisdom that Christian leaders pursued in their desire to sustain spiritual health. In the history of the church, this ministry was referred to as "spiritual direction." It was now clear that I needed someone who could help me make sense of the events of my life and the impact they were having on my soul. I needed a place to ask my questions, read my journal entries, shed my tears, pray, and rediscover God in the middle of the mess. I needed someone who would help me discern God's voice in the dramatic highs and lows of life and ministry. I began the search for a spiritual director, or what many people call a "soul friend."

Looking back, my decision to seek out a spiritual director was one that would forever alter the way I pursue spiritual growth and the way I engage in ministry with others. It was a decision that ultimately led to writing this book. I write believing there is a critical need for Christian leaders to recover this long-lost practice. Since I arrived at this conviction, I am discovering more and more people who see the value of this spiritual discipline. They, too, are exploring the hidden treasure of spiritual direction. A *soul companion* has joined them in discerning where and how God is at work in "the good, the bad, and the ugly." As Paula D'Arcy has said, "God comes to you disguised as your life." Spiritual direction becomes the sacred place where we discover his presence.

An Underlying Conviction

Working with leaders has convinced me that there are many of us who unexpectedly find ourselves in places of brokenness, confusion, and disillusionment. Recently I sat with a very close friend and lead pastor in his mid-thirties. His church is doing well in *every* way.

However, at his pastoral staff meeting earlier that day he had broken down and reported "things are happening inside of me that never happened before." In tears, he admitted that the challenges were wearing him out. He needed to take a break before he went over the edge. I hear this same story over and over again as I move through the world of Christian leaders.

Ruth Barton, founder of the Transforming Center and spiritual director to other leaders writes:

> I am not the only leader to have come to spiritual direction by way of desperation. Many pastors and leaders come for spiritual direction because they, too, are experiencing inner emptiness in the midst of outward busyness, feeling "stuck" in their spiritual lives, or longing for more in the midst of seeming success. Their question is, where does a leader go to articulate questions that seem so dangerous and doubts that seem so unsettling? Who pastors the pastor? Who provides spiritual leadership for the leader? Often it is a spiritual director.[2]

This book is born out of a deep belief. Here it is: *I don't think spiritual direction is a specialized ministry for persons facing unique situations. I believe every leader needs a soul friend.* I'm not the only person who holds this conviction. Kenneth Leech authored the groundbreaking classic, *Soul Friend: Spiritual Direction in the Modern World*, more than thirty-five years ago. In the introduction to his book, Leech declares: "Spiritual direction must be reclaimed in the service of the kingdom of God."[3] And, just in case we don't get the message, on the first page of his book we find only one line—an old Celtic saying: "Anyone without a soul friend is a body without a head." That might seem overstated to you. However, as we work our way through the following chapters, I believe it might actually begin to make sense.

I'm fifty-eight years old and have spent more than thirty-five of those years in ministry. Recently someone asked me to speak on the topic "What Would You Do Different If You Were Starting Over Again?" Of course, there are several things I would want to say, but I definitely have a bottom line that comes out of my life experience after all these years: "Everyone needs spiritual direction. Everyone needs a soul friend."

This conviction actually goes back almost 2,000 years when early Christians began to see the need for guidance amid all the challenges of spiritual living in a pagan world. So what's changed over two millennia? Nothing! We still need guides—people who will help us discover where Christ is at work amid the highs and lows of our life and leadership.

Maybe you were drawn to this book because the concept of spiritual direction recently moved onto your radar and you want to learn more. You've heard about these things and are wondering if there is anything in it for you. There is. Not because I said so, but because the church has been saying so for centuries. We lost the message and it's time to recover it!

If I could go back thirty-five years, I would do a number of things differently. But, this much I know for sure: I would not push through the challenges of ministry without a spiritual guide. So I have a bottom line as I write this book. The old Celtic saying is a bit shocking, but we need to unpack it: "Anyone without a soul friend is a body without a head."

I am sure there are many reasons why I wound up in the psychiatrist's office on that difficult day almost ten years ago.

One of them was this: I had traversed too much territory without interpretation. While I had many friends, I didn't have a soul friend, someone who knew how to truly listen to the Holy Spirit while they listened to me. Someone who knew how to discern my heart, ask good questions, and gently offer guidance—the kind of guidance that would shape my spiritual journey by opening doors and entering rooms I didn't know existed.

When my boat landed on the rocks, I discovered that I was blind to a lot of things. Despite all of my "success" in ministry, I was out of touch with myself and, though I had sincerely wanted to grow spiritually (and believed I loved God deeply), I was out of touch with God in those unopened areas of my life.

My guess is that your world isn't much different than mine when it comes to the truth we don't know about ourselves. You probably won't wind up in a psychiatrist's office as the motivating experience that moves you to take an interest in spiritual direction. But, if you're willing, I'd like to gently push you over the edge. *Leaders need soul friends!* So come with me on an exploratory journey to see if there might be something worth discovering.

Reading with the End in Mind

It will help you to know where we are going before you read the pages that follow. Let's begin by answering a fundamental question: *Is this book for ministry leaders who want to learn more about spiritual direction, or is it for people who are spiritual directors and want to learn more about how to help leaders in ministry?* The answer to that is: both. I trust I have written this in such a way that this material will be helpful on either side of the fence.

If you are investigating spiritual direction for the first time, I believe this book will provide a solid understanding, helping you determine how this ministry fits in your life. I am convinced that spiritual direction holds a very important place in forming your soul! Additionally, your role as a Christian leader puts you in the unique position of guiding others spiritually. While you may never become a certified spiritual director, this book will offer insights into how you can lead others with greater care. I believe these insights are critical for all Christian leaders.

On the other hand, if you are already a spiritual director involved in guiding others, I believe this book will present an essential window into the world of the leader, increasing your effectiveness as you relate to this distinctive group of people. Leaders live in a unique situation, one that complicates their spiritual journey. They need guides who understand their world, guides who demonstrate compassion, wisdom, and discernment.

My goal in writing is to help you explore various aspects of spiritual direction, and I conclude with a focus on the personal application of this spiritual practice in your life. Our starting point is the current landscape of ministry as we address the question: Why is there a surging need for spiritual direction among leaders? Then, I'll define and outline the nature of spiritual guidance so you have a clear idea of what this practice is all about. At this point we will dig into the theological and biblical foundations of this ministry. Midway into the book we'll take an extended look at Ignatius of Loyola, a sixteenth century leader, who shaped the world of spiritual direction by developing a ministry plan that is still used to this day. My goal in highlighting his life and teachings will be to draw out the time-tested, invaluable practices he developed and taught. Then we'll move to the present day and consider the principles that are surfacing in the contemporary world of spiritual direction.

There will be one more chapter—a critical one. My prayer is that this book will shape your journey in two ways that are highlighted in the final chapter.

First, when you conclude reading, you may want to find a spiritual director—someone who has learned the art of soul care through training and one-to-one experience. My goal will be to assist you in knowing how to seek out the right person as your spiritual director, someone who will function as a soul friend to you as a leader. I have already told you how spiritual direction came to play a critical role in my life. I continue to meet monthly with my director, believing this is an integral aspect of my ongoing pursuit of spiritual health. Possibly you will come to the same conclusion.

Second, I will introduce you to something called "group spiritual direction" ("group" means as few as two and not more than five or six people). This type of direction is mutual in that the members of the group provide guidance for one another. Group direction is easily implemented and profoundly transformational. My goal will be to help you understand the nature of this approach and assist you in taking the necessary steps to get started. I am personally engaged in group direction on a regular basis with a number of other leaders. It plays a vital role, catalyzing spiritual formation in my life each time we meet. Group spiritual direction is an easy entry point for those who see the value of this practice.

At the end of each chapter I have included a short, personal story of how spiritual direction has impacted the life of a leader. Think of these vignettes as windows into one person's journey revealing the value and influence of spiritual guide.

So there you have it. *I believe that if every leader were regularly engaged in some form of spiritual direction, the ministry landscape would look significantly different.* I care deeply about leaders and my present career in ministry takes me into your world on a daily basis. I think spiritual direction will play a central role in forming your soul and leading you to sustainable and joyful ministry patterns.

Let the journey begin . . .

2

It's Not Optional:
Why Spiritual Direction Matters

When Ministry Becomes High-Risk

The need to recover the practice of spiritual direction—once well established in the church—becomes obvious in light of the increasing challenges faced in the world of ministry, coupled with the spiritual and emotional impact those challenges have on Christian leaders. More and more men and women are losing their way as a result of the unchecked stress fostered by the overwhelming expectations—whether real or perceived—that are placed on them. The normal ministry responsibilities have been significantly compounded by the surge in programmatic and executive functions that now dominate the job description. It is becoming painfully obvious that many leaders are unable to sustain these escalating challenges in the complicated world of overseeing a ministry.

I have discovered that Christian organizations, both inside and outside of the church, are often characterized by systemic patterns that put the leader at risk. If you are approaching this book as a parachurch leader, or possibly a business executive, I am confident you will find most everything I address will apply in your context. I have worked in both organizational worlds—inside the church and alongside the church. My current work as the executive director of *SoulFormation* puts me in contact with pastors, parachurch leaders, missionaries, and business leaders. In my opinion, we are all in the same boat, and the rocky shore is not far away!

So what do I mean by the "rocky shore"? An email landed in my inbox some time ago. The thoughts expressed by this young leader are ones that provide a backdrop to the issues faced by all Christian leaders. Here is what I read:

> I believe I am in need of some soul care. I know we all struggle with different issues in ministry from time to time. I certainly do. But I think some of my issues have been piling up so much that I am at a point where I'm ready to throw in the "ministry towel." I really don't want to continue serving unless God changes my heart. I think all the issues I'm struggling with stem from my heart condition. I don't know how to heal/fix/mend it myself. . . . My wife has been telling me that I need to find a "spiritual director."

He ends by asking, "Can you steer me to someone who can help me sift through the mess my heart is in right now?" The driving concern reflected by this email is obvious. How do we nurture the spiritual and emotional health of leaders long before they reach this level of internal disillusionment? How do we cultivate ways of relational care that foster spiritual well-being amid the challenges of ministry, ways that result in sustainable and joyful service? Was Jesus giving us the straight truth when he said, "My yoke is easy and my burden is light"? I regularly work with people who secretly feel this promise is out of reach! The overwhelming nature of their world had led them to conclude that such a hope-filled experience is unrealistic.

Before we can consider pathways to health, it is necessary to start with the truth about ministry: Leadership comes with occupational hazards. We must face the primary contributors to the at-risk nature of Christian leadership in today's world. So, let's begin by naming the primary hazards that ministry leaders deal with on a day-to-day basis.

1. **Unrealistic Responsibilities**: The job of the ministering person is never finished. David Olsen and William Grosch, in an article entitled *Clergy Burnout: A Self Psychology and Systems Perspective* highlight the tendency to overwork in the ministry:

> Clergy burnout is a concern of all religious denominations. Meeting the constant demands of visitation, pastoral counseling, administration, preaching, teaching, facilitating church growth, as well as being expected to be an expert in crisis intervention, leaves many clergy feeling inadequate, exhausted, frustrated, and frequently questioning their call to ministry.[1]

There are simply too many important responsibilities within the leader's job description. Additionally, in most settings, these expectations are implied and rarely written down—they fall into the category marked "immeasurable." Over time, leaders often wonder if they're making a difference in the face of all of the energy they expend. The risk of becoming disillusioned, and even embittered, runs high for the leader who rarely experiences positive feedback or encouragement.

These unrealistic responsibilities have led many leaders to a very dangerous place as the temptation to work harder consumes them while the outcome they desire remains unattainable. In so doing, they allow the world of ministry to run them over; to convince them that self-care is unnecessary. They ignore a basic principle: When ministry demands go up, the need for soul-care also increases. Leaders easily fall into a compulsive pattern of drivenness as they become enmeshed in the world of ministry and the demands it places on them.

In working with Christian leaders I often throw a question at them: "You love what you're doing, but you simply can't keep doing it this way . . . right?" Or, I say, "You love what you're doing, but it's killing you . . . right?" The response is almost always the same. I have touched the core issue: They love the ministry, but at the same time, they feel overwhelmed by the treadmill effect that begins to impact the soul.

2. **Emotional Drain**: I regularly meet leaders whose emotional gauge is on empty. It has been there for months . . . even years! The truth is that it's very difficult to keep any emotional equilibrium in a world where one is celebrating births, mourning deaths, nurturing marriages, advising parents, confronting divorce, and counseling individuals in crisis. If you are a teaching pastor, you carry the added weight of preparing and delivering a message, sometimes multiple times on a weekend. Whether working one-to-one or speaking to a large group, leaders feel the weight of shepherding a flock where every individual is making decisions with eternal implications. It shouldn't surprise us that most leaders feel emotionally depleted—their tank is empty and knowing how to fill it seems out of reach.

One individual expressed himself to me by saying: "I feel like I am an ATM—I am being hit up for withdrawals constantly and very few people make a deposit. . . . Very few people understand these demands and the importance of disengagement from ministry to care for my own soul." This individual is saying what every leader must learn—the reality that emotional drain will sweep you off your feet if you don't develop a strategy to care for your own soul. The relational demands of ministry are relentless. They just keep coming!

• I remember stepping off the stage on a Sunday morning only to be informed that a drunk driver had killed Cal, my dear friend and fellow elder. His daughter died the next day.

• I remember the deep pain I felt when a long term leader and friend left the church over the position we reached regarding the role of women in ministry.

• I remember looking at a key church leader as we sat in my driveway after a difficult meeting. I said, "I need your help and I need you now." Nothing changed.

• I remember dedicating a baby at the hospital, knowing that we were preparing for impending death, not celebrating life.

• I remember learning that one of our staff counselors was sexually involved with a client and we were in a lawsuit, one that lasted two years and cost our insurance company close to a quarter of a million dollars to settle.

• I remember conducting the funeral of a young man who loved God, but, in a moment of despair, blew his head off with a shotgun.

• I remember sitting with a married couple as the husband informed his wife that he was in an affair that subsequently blew up their marriage. There was no guilt or shame as he described his total loss of integrity.

• I remember advising fellow staff members (who were good friends) that they should resign because support for their leadership had eroded.

• I remember sitting with a friend and pastor on our team a few days before Christmas as the police chaplain informed him that his son had overdosed on heroin.

• I remember struggling with what the doctor finally categorized as "chronic fatigue" while I continued to face the weekly demands of ministry, concluding each weekend by preaching four times.

The unique nature of ministry is that you don't have time to process the emotional highs and lows before the next one lands in your life.

What do you remember? Stop and name them... one, two, three, four. When you begin to track them you discover something: The emotional demands continue to roll into your world unannounced. And there is never enough time to celebrate the highs, or grieve the lows, of these traumatic events. What actually requires days and weeks to process often gets only a few hours.

It goes like this: On the same day you have the indescribable joy of leading someone into the kingdom of God, you hear of an affair, a death, a conflict, a betrayal. There are no guidelines to process the emotional swings of leadership; they come unannounced, and so rapidly, that you have no time to adapt or recover. Emotional drain isn't just a part of the job . . . it's the painful part of the job that's never-ending.

3. **Spiritual Neglect**: In the face of the increasing responsibilities, and the resulting emotional drain, many leaders struggle to find time to care for their own spiritual health. When I asked how ministry pressures were affecting him, one colleague wrote, "When I get weary of 'spiritual work,' I'm not easily drawn to the spiritual disciplines to refresh myself . . . There doesn't seem to be emotional energy or reserve to pursue God."

Many leaders indicate that they feel a resistance toward prayer and other spiritual disciplines in the middle of their busy world, even though they know this is the pathway to health. They find themselves edging away from the places that lead to personal renewal and wholeness. As I minister to leaders I am discovering a dangerous pattern—many of them have no practices of spiritual renewal built into their lives. In their week-to-week schedule, they overlook the necessity of prayer, scripture, solitude, and Sabbath.

As contradictory as it seems, many leaders have no sacred rhythms in their own world.

I recently connected with a pastor who told me he simply could not preach one more message. He felt a profound sense of hollowness and deep disillusionment had captured his inner core. He then said, "I feel like I have tended to my professional development over the years but have failed to care for my own soul while in the ministry." The situation had reached such a high level of ambiguity that my counsel was painful but necessary: "You need to leave the ministry so you can discover God again." He resigned.

If you are failing to feed your soul, while at the same time you are handling sacred responsibilities, the disconnect will finally become too much. The only way we can remain integrated in ministry is to follow Jesus' pattern—"listen to the Father." Those who press on in ministry, while at the same time allowing their inner life to slip into disrepair, are living a contradiction. A critical part of their personhood falls out of alignment. Sooner or later they *dis-integrate*. A leader caves in because the soul simply cannot bear the weight of ministry while neglecting those rhythms that foster intimate union with God.

4. **Relational Isolation**: Ministry has another occupational hazard—the tendency toward isolation. This is often the case at the very time a leader needs emotional and spiritual support from others. In surveying pastors within my denomination I discovered that fifty percent do not have someone they consider a close friend. In surveys done by other organizations that number goes as high as seventy percent.[2]

I recently conducted a soul-care seminar with pastors. The conversation was engaging and honest. Finally, one of the seasoned leaders in the room despondently expressed, "No man cares for my soul." His comment triggered an immediate sense of deep concern in my heart. We made an appointment to talk and he informed me of how a church member had violated one of his children. The shameful indiscretion should have resulted in church discipline against the perpetrator, but instead led to a decision by the pastor to leave the church he loved. He had carried this pain in isolation . . . grief that had been lodged for years. Following the seminar, I found the reference he was referring to when he spoke up. He quoted Psalm 142:4: "I looked on my right hand, and beheld, but there was no man that would know me: refuge failed me; no man cared for my soul" (KJV).

Leaders often experience a sense of brokenness in dramatic ways, yet the culture of ministry makes it very difficult to reveal this neediness to others. Some of the confirming statements made to me include: "My failures are not safe to share. My attempts at being the so called 'authentic, transparent leader' are always met by elders with looks of concern." Another wrote, "The challenge to be transparent and honest is one that I've struggled with. Will people allow me to be honest?"

Speaking for myself, when I "hit the wall," I was simply too ashamed to let others know the depth of my interior crisis. I had lots of close friends and ministry colleagues who loved me. Yet, in the middle of the crisis I pulled inward and tried to hold it together. I didn't know how to process the frustration and failure. I was isolated!

5. **Identity Issues**: Often, the at-risk nature of ministry is increased by the leader's failure to develop a strong sense of self in his or her early years. I have observed that a particularly high number of people who enter the ministry remain oblivious to unresolved issues surrounding their identity—issues that frequently are connected to their family of origin. These areas of unresolved need result in adaptive patterns (or ways of being) that are developed in an attempt to protect oneself from a world that failed to love them unconditionally. Sadly, these childhood patterns

of survival are then linked to the development of a false self (or shadow) that shapes the way the leader functions later in life.

Robert Johnson contends that these "refused and unacceptable characteristics do not go away; they only collect in the dark corners of our personality. When they have been hidden long enough, they take on a life of their own, the shadow life."[3] Furthermore, this false self is usually embedded in such a way that it becomes particularly difficult to identify, let alone address and resolve.

Robert Mulholland states, "When we live as a false self we fear that our lack of a true center for our identity will be revealed and that weakness exploited by others. One of the ways our false self tries to compensate is to find our identity in performance."[4] Hence, the motives driving the ministry are tainted in a way that results in the leader expending unnecessary energy to meet the expectations of others. In my own experience, I failed to see that my journey into anxiety and depression was directly linked to the ways in which I connected self-worth and identity to an unhealthy need for affirmation. Unknowingly, this faulty motivation compromised my ability to lead others in a healthy manner, especially when the going got rough. It's easy to lose your balance when your identity is not properly grounded in God.

I had a dark corner—a room I did not know existed. It wasn't until I transitioned into the difficult ministry I described that I was forced to face my codependent leadership pattern. I had always been able to keep people happy. Yet, I never realized why I had developed this skill to such a high level. Underneath, I was motivated by a deep need to be needed, wanted, praised, and loved. In the end, it was this twisted motivation that pushed me over the edge. Quite simply, I felt like I had "prostituted" myself . . . I gave up my emotional boundaries in an attempt to keep others happy. I discovered how high the cost can be when people-pleasing becomes addictive. In the end, my letter of resignation had to be written. There was no other way to recover.

Every leader has identity issues that drive the false self. The real question is whether those issues are being brought into the light. If not, they continue to gather strength underground.

For reasons stated above, and many others that could be explored, Christian leaders are truly at-risk—not only in their professions, but also in their personal spiritual journeys. Most people enter the ministry with extremely high ideals, only to find that after laboring over an extended period of time, there is an ever-widening, huge gulf between their level of expectation and the actual results.

I recently met with one pastor (we'll call him Mike) who oversees a large and, what seems to be, healthy church. My regular contact with Mike left me assured that he was on top of his world. His emotional health seemed strong, and I certainly viewed him as someone who was not in the at-risk category.

However, shortly after I made this optimistic assumption about Mike, I met with him only to find out that he'd had a dramatic meltdown the Sunday before. It was the beginning of a new year and he was preaching a series on vision. On this particular Sunday, Mike was making a point from Galatians 6:9, "Be not weary in doing good," as a way to stir the congregation to greater commitment. When these words left his mouth, he stopped short and then began to weep uncontrollably. Mike was unable to collect himself despite several attempts. The experience continued for about five minutes. Finally, some church leaders came to the pulpit to offer support so he could bring the service to a conclusion.

When we met for our time of spiritual direction, Mike indicated that he had no idea the meltdown was imminent in his life. All he knew was that when the words "be not weary in doing good" left his mouth, a tsunami surged in his own soul. *He was weary amid the responsibilities—weary in a way that he had somehow been avoiding all along.*

Like Mike, many leaders are functioning in a manner that is simply not sustainable. Something is fundamentally wrong but remains unnoticed and unaddressed.

Systemic Issues Increase the Danger

We have looked at five occupational hazards in ministry, ones that can sabotage the leader before she or he fully realizes what has happened. If leaders are honest, many of them will say, "I simply can't keep doing it this way!" Yet, this feeling in the leader's soul often fails to be articulated. It begs for attention but gets none. There are many people who never address the soul-care issues necessary to secure the kind of health needed to lead well. Failing here, we fail everywhere.

All of this raises the question: Are there systemic issues infecting Christian organizations that fuel the dangerous slide toward spiritual and emotional disillusionment in the life of the leader? From my perspective, the answer to this is obvious. Leaders of Christian ministries easily lose sight of spiritual formation in favor of other attractions that are fostered within the organizational culture. Unless the systemic dysfunction is named and addressed, the leader will function in a structure that continually undermines sustainable and joyful service.

Allow me to walk you through a list of assumptions. If these statements are true, then the very culture in which Christian leaders work is at cross-purposes with the inner wholeness they so deeply need and desire. Sadly, I suspect the statements that follow are descriptive of most organizations. It's a dangerous slide:

1. *Consumer Culture:* Leading a ministry in a consumer culture where "attractional strategies" and "measurable results" dominate the landscape makes it very difficult to prioritize and strategize the ongoing work of spiritual formation. The slow work of transformation is preempted by numerical and programmatic success. Many leaders, and the organizations in which they work, have become addicted to "bigger is better." The need to achieve results assumes an idolatrous hold on the leader's soul. Few people would dispute that we have made measurable success the primary goal that drives the ministry agenda.

2. *Employment and Performance:* In our consumer culture, outcomes are directly connected to an employment strategy where leaders are managed and evaluated by goals and objectives. Either directly or indirectly, leaders discover that the bottom line is performance, effectiveness, and accomplishment. Without realizing it, that mentality asks the leader to operate according to a "scorecard" that overlooks their need for soul-care. The spiritual maturity and nurture of the leader is assumed to be of crucial importance, yet nothing is put in place to cultivate and secure this as a primary outcome. The focus of the organization is squarely placed on external performance. Internal health (spiritual and emotional well-being) is rarely discussed or intentionally nurtured.

3. *Management Trumps Mystery:* The slide continues as the primary ministry strategy is built around thinking, planning, and action that is focused and organized around programmatic models and tactics. The leader comes to believe that "being is doing" and gives up mystery for management. As long as this approach is working—and the faulty definition of success is achievable—the leader is affirmed and continues to put his or her eggs in this basket. This can go on for years before a backlash occurs and the leader realizes he or she is on a collision course with disaster.

4. *Relational Trust Is Lost:* In a performance-oriented system, trust and deep relationships are unintentionally traded for results. We say we are in community, but the authenticity needed for such depth is often superseded by the need to succeed and look good. When this happens, leaders are no longer functioning in a place of emotional safety and transparency. They experience a "disconnect" from the very people they serve. True community has become fatally compromised in the life of the very person who leads the community. If you talk to many leaders you will find that there is a deep longing for authentic relationships but an apparent inability to establish them.

5. *Compulsive Ministry Patterns:* When the leader becomes defined by what they do (and not who they are), they often succumb to insecurity, drivenness, and faulty motivation in ministry. At this point, he or she is no longer living into their true calling and turns to patterns of pleasing and the need to succeed as a way to find the affirmation they long for. Instead of listening to the Father (as was modeled for us by Jesus), they listen to myriad other voices that feed their identity and ministry direction.

6. *God Is Gone and Pressure Is On:* When spiritual formation is no longer at the center—when mystery gives way to management—leaders lose the art of spiritual discernment. They resort to business models of decision-making. We seek to find answers to problems through data, analysis, our own wisdom, and self-effort rather than prayer and dependency on God. In the end, the ministry becomes a man-made system that is overly dependent on one person to keep it going—the person in charge. At this point, the at-risk nature of the work begins to bear down on the leader and the outcome takes them to places they never anticipated.

If you work under the assumptions stated above, a time will come when ministry no longer holds the luster it once had. Sooner or later, many people in ministry begin to feel resistance toward that which originally was their calling and an exciting vision. *The systemic issue is clear: The culture in which Christian leaders serve is prone to steer them toward the pursuit of career dreams and ministry ideals for the wrong reasons.* To avert the associated dangers, something needs to be in place long before this misdirection sets in. The leader is in need of a spiritual guide who will lovingly help them process their union with Christ amid the dangers that ministry exerts on the soul.

The Need for Spiritual Direction

In her book, *Learning to Lead from Your Spiritual Center*, Patricia Brown succinctly points out why leaders need to become aware of the spiritual issues in their own lives before seeking to help others:

> The failure of leaders to deal with their own souls, their inner life, is deeply troubling not only for themselves but also for other persons in the misery they cause. The destructive consequences from leaders who fail to work out of a deep sense of their inner self are staggering. . . . Leaders have a particular responsibility to know what is going on inside their souls.[5]

Most Christian leaders make the faulty assumption that they can pastor or shepherd themselves. They believe that since all the members of their community look to them for spiritual leadership, they must also be qualified to effectively tend their own souls. Assuming this autonomous pathway is always dangerous.

It is important to note that the very people we lead reinforce the distortions found in the leader's thinking. They encourage the leader to function as an isolated hero who has no specialized need for soul care.

We must realize that the "professional" ministry leader is no different from other professionals (such as lawyers or physicians) when it comes to receiving what they give. We would never expect a doctor to diagnose and treat his or her own disease, or an attorney to represent themselves in their personal litigation. It is standard practice that those who work with people are expected to place themselves under the guidance of others when it comes to personal issues triggered by their professional work. Yet, most Christian leaders naïvely assume that they can "doctor" themselves without the help of others.

It is also tempting for leaders to think that the structures of the church or Christian organization will somehow provide the spiritual and emotional support they need. Such an assumption places the leader at risk. It is highly unlikely that the spiritual enrichment and accountability needed to sustain the leader will come solely from within. Yet, most leaders never think to seek out a spiritual director or counselor who will listen to their deepest questions, ministry disappointments, or emotional pain.

Roy Oswald, a senior consultant with the Alban Institute, has extensive experience in working with pastors. In his book, *Clergy Self-Care*, he emphasizes this sad reality: "The majority of clergy I work with have no one who relates to them in this special way, no one who pays particular attention to them and their spiritual journey and with whom they regularly review their spiritual path."[6] He also says, "If I were to choose one discipline to undergird all others, it would be meeting regularly with a spiritual director."[7]

This lone ranger approach to the spiritual journey has not always been the case. In the history of the church, pastors were encouraged to have a spiritual companion. Eugene Peterson, whose writings offer much wisdom to ministry leaders, states:

> For a long time in the church's life, people expected that the pastor, one entrusted to give personal and detailed guidance to people journeying and growing in the way of faith, would be provided with an equivalent guidance. Having a spiritual director, whether called by that name or not, was assumed in the job description.[8]

In his own journey toward spiritual direction, Peterson says, "I also knew that in other [Christian] traditions it was unthinkable for persons who had any kind of leadership responsibilities in the life of prayer to proceed without a spiritual director."[9] He goes on to lament that in the ministry today, we rarely find a pastor who has a spiritual director. Many Christian leaders are even suspicious of the concept since such a discipline is foreign to their religious tradition.

To counter this dangerous pattern, a serious attempt must be made to introduce (or re-introduce) Christian leaders to the need and value of spiritual direction. In recent years, many have discovered the value of this ministry and are quick to affirm the awakening. More and more leaders are realizing there is great value in having a spiritual director or soul friend who will help them discover God's fingerprints in the middle of life's complexities. The beginning stages of this rediscovery offer a ray of hope that this practice will spread into the mainstream of Christian leadership.

As I look back on the day when the words, "I have totally and completely lost my way," came from my lips in the psychiatrist's office, I am able to see the beginning of God's good work in my life. In the middle of my pain was his call to discover an ancient discipline—one that I wish had been in place years before.

A Spiritual Direction Story
Jeff Wiesinger – A Pastor

I am the pastor of a church of 150 people in Anchorage, Alaska. It was six years ago that I had reached a place of despair. I was carrying out ministry responsibilities out of willful duty, knowing that the things I said and did were true, but enjoying none of the personal experience of God that I spoke of so often. After months of pleading, my wife, now in tears, was begging me to call our denominational office. My pride finally succumbed to her tears and I made the call. Through district leadership, I was connected with an individual who would function as my spiritual director. This began a six-year relationship that has been a steadily refining journey.

Frequently our dialogues were questions of core motivations, of what really drove me in life and in ministry. It became apparent that wrestling with my inner life was going to be necessary and this would lead to discovering my area of greatest struggle. The process allowed God to "help" me understand the condition of my own heart, but I was determined to keep final authority in both who I was and what I was going to do about it. When asked by my director if I believed in Step One of the Twelve Steps: "My life was unmanageable, and was I powerless to change it," I was immediate in my response. "No, I can do this!" I was a helpless perfectionist.

Early on in life, after a series of continuing losses, I concluded that no one was ultimately trustworthy with the condition of my heart. Even after my conversion as a teenager, while I was immensely grateful for God's forgiveness, I lived every day as if my salvation depended on me. Life, especially ministry, became an exhausting journey of doing what everyone on the outside thought was best, but all the while sinking deeper into the abyss. And now I was finally crashing, arriving at the place where God might reach me. I began to take time to listen, to journal, to open my heart and mind to what he wanted to say to me.

As I processed things with my director, he offered open-ended questions revealing God's heart for me—not the pastor, but the one whom Christ loved. Several breakthroughs came over the years, but I still look back wistfully and realize that my tendency was to allow each moment of Spirit-directed revelation become a new insight by which I could finally live life the "right" way.

A circumstantially difficult nine-month season of ministry brought me once again to a place of soul weariness. I reentered a season of deep discouragement, even as my director continued to gently nudge me into places of solitude, asking me to readdress truths God had spoken to me about where my identity truly lay.

During a walk at a retreat center, I cried out to heaven, "I can't do this anymore." What descended upon me in that moment was the deepest awareness of my sin I had ever known. I was sinful to the core, and there was nothing I could do to change that. All this in a manner of seconds, and yet immediately, the overwhelming flood of his grace washed over me, and I reflected: *So this is what the peace that passes all understanding feels like.* Years of spiritual direction, gentle questions, fierce challenges, and loving support had led me to the place where I could receive the truth of sin's dark depths—and grace's greater depth.

3

Lost and Found:
Recovering the Art of Spiritual Direction

What Is Spiritual Direction?

I remember the first time I walked into the office of my spiritual director and wondered exactly what the experience would be like. I had read books by leading Christian authors who mentioned spiritual direction, but I really had no working knowledge of what this spiritual discipline might involve. In fact, it remained kind of mysterious, and it was this uncertainty that kept me on the outside and looking in for such a long time.

Before I offer a definition for this ministry, it might be helpful to clarify a misconception around the terms "spiritual direction" and "director." These words feel authoritarian, as if the directee is being managed or controlled. However, "direction" simply refers to the end goal of time spent together—that the directee would have a sense of direction, insight, or discernment from God in her or his life. The director guides the process, but would never assume control. He or she functions as a spiritual companion. In the end, it is the Holy Spirit who directs, as together we listen for God's promptings. Understood this way, the spiritual director acts humbly as God's facilitator on behalf of someone who seeks to grow in grace.

Various definitions have been offered to explain spiritual

direction. Eugene Peterson simply states: "Spiritual direction takes place when two people agree to give their full attention to what God is doing in one (or both) of their lives and seek to respond in faith."[1] In *The Practice of Spiritual Direction,* a contemporary classic written by William A. Barry and William J. Connolly, we find this:

> We define Christian spiritual direction, then, as help given by one Christian to another which enables that person to pay attention to God's personal communication to him or her, to respond to this personally communicating God, to grow in intimacy with this God, and to live out the consequences of the relationship.[2]

If we consider these and other definitions of spiritual direction, we discover two features are central to the nature and practice of this discipline. First, it involves an attempt to listen to another person for the purpose of helping that individual recognize and discern God's movement in his or her life. Listening to God, and to the other, is fundamental to the process of discovering how Christ is present.

Second, spiritual direction is primarily focused on the directee's experience and not on ideas or speculative theology. The purpose of direction is to foster a more personal or intimate union with God, one that is relational in the fullest sense of the term. It is the inner experience or emotional awareness that becomes the framework for discovery together. Both of these emphases, *one-to-one listening* and *personal experience*, will be explored extensively in the chapters that follow.

Henri Nouwen believed that spiritual direction can be defined as a "relationship initiated by a spiritual seeker who finds a mature person of faith willing to pray and respond with wisdom and understanding to his or her questions about how to live spiritually in a world of ambiguity and distraction."[3] I like those words "how to live spiritually in a world of ambiguity and distraction." We need all the help we can get if we desire to integrate our Christian faith into our life in today's world. Nouwen believed that a soul friend is critical if we hope to survive the challenges and questions that following Christ will bring.

Spiritual Direction – An Ancient Discipline

Now that we know what we mean by the term "spiritual direction," let's take a brief look at the historical development of this spiritual exercise. In seeking to build a rationale for this ministry of care, we must look back in the history of the church. When we do this, we discover patterns that affirm the practice and importance of spiritual direction. Looking back is necessary because, as in all areas of church life—whether it is doctrine or practice—we take needless risks when we overlook what our spiritual fathers and mothers have already learned. Kenneth Leech reminds us:

A closer look at the lives of holy men and women throughout the history of Christianity shows us that those who searched with great fervor for an intimate relationship with God always asked for guidance and direction. Those who searched for God in the Egyptian deserts of many centuries ago, as well as those who search for him in Calcutta, Tokyo, or New York, have in common the desire for someone to guide them through the wilderness of inner and outer experience.[4]

Our journey takes us all the way back to the early church fathers (Tertullian, Cyprian, Ambrose, and Jerome), whose words and correspondence (they often wrote letters) demonstrate the direction of particular individuals under their care.[5] Saint Augustine (354–430), the great theologian of the fourth century, emphasized that "no one can walk without a guide."[6] It was during this time that spiritual direction was shaped by the Desert Fathers and Mothers within the communities that formed in the Egyptian desert. John Cassian (350–435) is noted as the first individual who, having been influenced by the desert ascetics, developed an intentional process of spiritual care by placing every novice under the guidance of an older monk. Gerald May highlights this:

In Christianity, formal individual spiritual direction is usually seen as having begun in the third and fourth centuries, when many individuals sought guidance from desert hermits. Thereafter, the spread of monasticism had a tremendous influence in refining and promulgating a variety of spiritual guidance traditions.[7]

In Ireland, we find that spiritual direction flourished as far back as the sixth century when missionary work expanded into this region. In the ancient Celtic church, a person who acted as a spiritual guide was called an *anam cara*, meaning "friend of the soul" or simply "soul friend." The *anam cara* was "a person to whom you could reveal the hidden intimacies of your life. This friendship was an act of recognition and belonging. When you had an *anam cara*, your friendship cut across all convention and category. You were joined in an ancient and eternal way with the friend of your soul."[8]

As we study history, other references to the practice of spiritual direction are found throughout the ancient Christian world. Saint Symeon, an eleventh century Eastern monk wrote, "Therefore, so that I may speak as if I had only one listener, here is what I will tell you; Brother, invoke God with persistence, in order that He might show you a person capable of guiding you well."[9]

I especially appreciate the words of Aelred of Rievaulx (1109–1166), an English monk who wrote, "What happiness, what security, what joy to have someone to whom you dare to speak on terms of equality . . . one to whom you need have no fear to confess your failings, one to whom you can unblushingly make known what progress you have made in the spiritual life."[10]

Stop and think about what it would mean to have that kind of spiritual friendship—someone who knows you so well, and loves you so sincerely, that you can process anything and everything in your journey.

Various women came to play a key role in the development of spiritual direction. Catherine of Sienna, a theologian in the fourteenth century, became a respected spiritual leader who offered guidance to both men and women. Her influence reached to the highest levels including the pope, to whom she wrote many letters.

Teresa of Avila (1515–1582) and St. John of the Cross (1542–1591) stand out as two of the leading figures in the history of spiritual direction. Teresa insisted that it is "a great advantage for us to be able to consult someone who knows us, so that we may learn to know ourselves."[11] St. John believed that "the soul needs spiritual guides that act as the gentle instruments of the Holy Spirit to lead us in our transformation in Christ."[12] These early church leaders offer an unusual and compelling legacy regarding the need for spiritual direction.

The seventeenth century was another high point in the historical development of spiritual guidance with such influential persons as Francis de Sales, Jane de Chantel, and Francois Fenelon. However, within Protestant circles a critical shift occurred at this time, and we discover a gap in the historical literature regarding the practice of spiritual direction.

This gap highlights the reason why the Protestant church is now looking for help as a desire is birthing to rediscover the lost art of spiritual direction. Roy Oswald, in his book, *How to Build a Support System for Your Ministry*, contends, "I believe we Protestant clergy do well to look within the Catholic tradition for persons with calling and skill in this vocation. The Roman Catholic church has a much longer tradition in spiritual direction than the Protestant church."[13]

How We Lost Spiritual Direction in the Protestant Tradition

Gerald May has addressed the loss of spiritual direction in his book, *Care of Mind/Care of Spirit*. He states, "Protestants have almost no tested and accepted methods of individual spiritual direction."[14] May contends:

> Amidst changing forms and emphases, Roman Catholic, Anglican, and Orthodox traditions have maintained some ongoing structures for spiritual direction. For Protestants, however, there have often been special theological problems with the idea of one person advising another on intimate matters of the spirit. Much of the concern here has to do with sacerdotalism, the possibility that the methods of personality of the spiritual director would supplant the role of Jesus as the prime mediator between God and the individual human being.[15]

When we study church history, it becomes clear that seeking the wisdom of a spiritual guide was lost in the early stages of the Protestant tradition. Forster Freeman contends that following the Reformation there were those who "abhorring Roman practices and fearful of clericalism, rejected such individual counsel while emphasizing the priesthood of all believers."[16]

James Houston underscores that the fear of Catholicism, and the tendency toward individualism, prevents Protestants from embracing spiritual direction:

> *Spiritual director, soul friend,* and *spiritual friendship*— these new buzz words in Protestant circles make us suspect someone has imported another fad from our society's "culture of novelty." Do they signal one

more encroachment on evangelical faith and practice? Some who are aware of these phrases' origins fear that "spiritual direction" is the Trojan horse of Catholicism.[17]

A dangerous assumption is embedded within the Protestant mind-set: Spirituality is individualistic in nature. One author, referencing the Protestant Reformation, called this assumption "a struggle for the irreplaceable individuality of the believer."[18]

The loss of spiritual direction in Protestant circles, and the resulting spiritual setback among leaders, would seem to be one of the major reasons why Christian leaders are now feeling the need to forge new pathways (or find lost ones) to enhance their own spiritual formation. Leighton Ford, long-time associate of Billy Graham, is one such evangelical who has felt a deep need for the recovery of spiritual direction and now gives most of his time to nurturing a few leaders.[19] Thankfully, this hunger appears to be on the increase and gives us hope that spiritual direction is in the early stages of rediscovery.

Jeannette Bakke, a leading author in this field, was interviewed by *Christianity Today* and asked, "Why is there a growing interest among Protestants and evangelicals in spiritual direction?" She answered:

People are hungry for authentic spiritual companionship. Many are concerned about the crassness of the larger culture, and the fracturedness and pace of life—they desire to slow down and notice more about who they are and how to be connected to God. They are dissatisfied with what feels like a lack of significance and are seeking something more.[20]

Spiritual companionship—certainly most Christian leaders hunger for friendship on this level. There is a deep thirst for soul friendships with few places to turn. What we now have is a shortage of spiritual guides when, at the same time, we are seeing more and more individuals looking for people who are trained in the art of spiritual direction. If we hope to see this ministry take hold as a widespread practice, then the need for more guides who offer this type of care must be addressed.

Regarding the lack of spiritual guidance in the current culture of church leaders, Kenneth Leech writes:

> It has not been obvious in recent decades that spiritual direction belongs to the core of the Christian ministry. . . . Those who have prepared for ministry over the last thirty or forty years learned much about the Bible, Church history, and Church doctrine, and sometimes also received good training in pastoral skills. But in the area of their personal relationship to God, most were left to their own devices and insights, and received virtually no guidance.[21]

In a survey of Christian leaders I asked this question: Was there a time when you experienced "spiritual direction" from someone else? One individual responded:

> I don't think I have ever experienced any kind of systematic spiritual direction from anyone in my life. . . . As I understand it, the basic question of spiritual direction is, "Where are you in relation to God right now?" I try to do this with my staff, but I don't have someone that does it with me. I would like a spiritual director.

Another wrote:

> I have never experienced a healthy mentoring relationship with any consistency or accountability. It would have helped me greatly, especially as a young pastor. And while my relationship with Christ has been good, I know it would have been healthier.

Such comments should stir a deep desire to restore the ministry of spiritual direction into the practices of today's Christian leaders. Yet, in most Christian communities, the need for a soul friend often goes unnoticed as we continue to labor in isolation.

In 1978 Richard Foster wrote *Celebration of Discipline* and opened a new way of understanding how we grow spiritually. In this wonderful book, he helped us see that ancient disciplines or rhythms were needed to secure an experiential and relational union with God. He touches down on the value of spiritual direction in his chapter on "Guidance." However, since Foster opened that door, scores of other books have been published on the topic of spiritual disciplines with an ever-expanding number of practices that deserve attention. *Yet, almost ALL of these books overlook spiritual direction!* That puzzles me! We fail to see the critical importance of one-to-one conversations that are transformational! We have lost an ancient discipline—the art of spiritual direction.

In the earliest stages of Christian thought and practice we find St. Augustine writing, "No one can walk without a guide." Twelve hundred years later St. Ignatius presses the value of soul friendship to the highest level and provides us with a guidebook, *The Spiritual Exercises*. And then comes the grand disconnect. Slowly but surely, Protestant individualism creates a type of spirituality that is void of soul companions. We journey alone. What's worse, we don't even know how to engage in truly deep conversations where we explore the depth of our hearts. The art of spiritual direction is like a lost language—few people know how to speak it any more. Recovery will require considerable work. Yet, it must be recovered for it is an original language; it is the language of the soul.

A Spiritual Direction Story
Shirley Kinsey – An Educator

"I always tell people who come to me to let me know if I say something insensitive." Margie spoke to a sanctuary-sized classroom filled with seminary students. A hush fell as her gentle voice settled into receptive minds. That was seven years ago and my first impression of her.

A year later, when I called the seminary to request spiritual directors with openings, they passed on Margie's name and number. Hoping, I placed the call. As a free gift of ministry, Margie offers spiritual friendship and guidance to twenty people. We arranged a session.

Leighton Ford says, "The heart of spiritual direction is helping the other person to listen and pay attention to what God is saying." Margie has mastered that. During an early visit, I explained my desire to pray continually but confessed that I found it challenging to the point of nearly impossible. She responded: "Let's pray silently together and listen to what God has to say. Pray aloud any time and close when you wish."

On another occasion, Margie listened attentively as I rattled on about my disappointment with a friend's choice to be unfaithful to her husband. I struggled with judging her actions, with my desire for a spirit of grace. This time she used questions to help me pay attention to God's voice: "What does God think of her recent actions? How does he feel about them? What is his approach as he desires her salvation and repentance?"

Considering God's perspective softened my heart toward my friend as I heard myself say that the Spirit of the Lord stays soft, ready to forgive and receive. She sprinkled questions amidst her listening. The fine wind of listening began to blow me in a new direction.

Recently, I climbed Margie's cracked cement steps, crossed the wide porch, and knocked. She seemed happy to see me. As she prepared tea in the kitchen, we chatted about a book on her counter, *Francis de Sales, Jane de Chantal: Letters of Spiritual Direction.* Both devoted readers, we often talk about books.

But once we entered the sunroom and settled in chairs and prayed, we focused on what has been happening between God and me. I told her that I've been thinking about a verse from Romans 15:7: "Accept one another, then, as Christ has accepted you, in order to bring praise to God." We agreed that accepting ourselves and accepting God's love precedes the acceptance of others. After hearing my difficulties forgiving myself for poor choices in my past, Margie explained to me the difference between guilt and shame.

Guilt, she said, is what we feel when we do something wrong. In contrast, shame is when we extend our guilt to define our character. If we tell a lie, we feel guilt. But if we extend our guilt by defining ourselves as liars, we move to shame. When we look back on our wayward past, it is best to say, "Even though I made some poor choices, my identity comes from how God sees me."

How does God see us? He delights in us because we belong to him and because he is strongly for us, wanting us—and guiding us when we listen—to make wise choices. I bounded down the steps from Margie's house after this discussion, smiling and ruminating on every word.

Once each month, I drive almost twenty miles to spend an hour or so with Margie. Sometimes, in sluggish traffic, I wonder why. Thomas Lewis, one of three psychiatrists who wrote *A General Theory of Love*, which is based on their studies of limbic resonance, explains it well yet not fully when he says: "About the only thing that makes people happy is spending time with people they are emotionally close with." Margie has nurtured an emotional and spiritual closeness that gives me deep joy.

4

Does the Bible Say Anything about Spiritual Direction?

It is clear that the ministry of spiritual direction has been off the radar in many Protestant Christian traditions for centuries. At the same time, the preceding chapters have established the growing need among Christian leaders to recover much-needed spiritual and emotional support by assisting them to discern and respond to God's work in their lives. The increasing complexities and demands of ministry only amplify the need for a soul friend. However, even though spiritual direction is gaining visibility as a valuable and necessary practice in the world of Christian leadership, a question remains in many people's minds: Is spiritual direction biblical?

When a particular spiritual discipline or practice (such as spiritual direction), disappears from the wider church over an extended period of time (several centuries), the total loss of awareness may lead to suspicion when the practice resurfaces. That which was once highly valued may seem odd and even theologically suspect. In recent years there have been numerous ancient practices, which, lost over time, have been reintroduced to the church: *lectio divina*, contemplative prayer, *examen*, a rule of life, and spiritual direction to name a few. Many Christian leaders experience an appropriate sense of caution surrounding practices that are foreign to their experience.

It is certainly wise to ask the question: "Is spiritual direction biblical?" After careful study, Gary Moon and David Benner make this response in their book, *Spiritual Direction and the Care of Souls*: "Without hesitation, yes! Scripture gives evidence of spiritual guidance in the time of Jesus and the earliest days of the Christian community. People were not just taught about the Way, they were helped to live in the Way."[1]

Before considering the biblical foundation, it is essential to recognize why the early church did not speak of spiritual direction as a distinct or specialized ministry in the way we know it today. Larry Crabb highlights this apparent silence: It is important to understand "that spiritual direction is never presented in the New Testament nor practiced in the early church as a profession. It is part of an organic community."[2]

Crabb contends that spiritual direction was "organic" in nature because it took place in the context of spiritual friendship—believers lived in ongoing fellowship together as "pastors, elders, and friends provided teaching, admonition, encouragement, and a collection of activities that can actually be called Spiritual Friendship and included Spiritual Direction."[3] This context changed when this unique pattern of community ended and believers were scattered into an unbelieving culture where they faced new challenges, temptations, and confusion regarding their spiritual journey. As a result, the need for spiritual guidance increased.

During the third century Desert Fathers and Mothers (hermits, ascetics, and monks) withdrew from a culture that was given to the pagan pursuit of pleasure. These Desert Saints longed for union with God in a context where solitude and prayer could be practiced free of distraction. As they cleared a pathway to God these men and women became the logical place to search for spiritual support. Spiritual seekers went to the desert in the pursuit of wisdom and guidance to assist them in their journey.

With this as a backdrop, we are ready to begin our study of the biblical and theological foundations for spiritual direction. To do so, we will start with the Trinitarian makeup of the godhead and the implications this carries for the Christian community and relational ministry within the body.

The Relational Nature of God

It is obvious that spiritual direction is highly relational in nature. The director and directee must dedicate themselves to trust, vulnerability, honesty, and a host of other interpersonal experiences. In our Western culture, characterized by an overriding attachment to individualism and independence, there are many people who fear spiritual intimacy, preferring to maintain—and even justify— some sense of detachment from others. Yet, it becomes very difficult to defend such a cautious approach to relationships in light of the remarkable interpersonal experiences Christ modeled and encouraged others to engage in. Jesus takes significant risks in his pursuit of relationships with others and then he chooses to process spiritual truths in the context of these friendships.

To understand the intentionality of Christ's relational example we must take a close look into the Trinitarian nature of God. In doing so, we discover Jesus' desire for community with others is actually a reflection of the community he experiences within the Trinity. The Father, Son, and Holy Spirit are inextricably bound together; they are defined by a relational dynamic, a distinguishing attribute that is passed on to each human being because we have been created in the image of God. Darrell Johnson states:

At the center of the universe is a relationship. This is the most fundamental truth I know. At the center of the universe is a community. It is out of that relationship that you and I were created and redeemed. And it is for that relationship that you and I were created and redeemed!

And it turns out that there is a threefoldness to that relationship. It turns out that the community is a Trinity. The center of reality is Father, Son and Holy Spirit.[4]

In recent years Christian leaders are rediscovering the doctrine of the Trinity and the implications for relational life and ministry together. One must ask why this theological truth is surfacing after being overlooked for so long. Is it not because our modern world drifted toward a culture of isolation, one that places the focus on success, materialism, and, ultimately, on an individualistic and an increasingly private way of life?

As individualism grew, it also shaped the church. Relational ministry, as exemplified by Christ, was lost in the midst of our busyness, and we unknowingly moved away from community as a defining mark. Sadly, church history will record the current generation as one characterized by a dramatic shift toward measurable programs and goal-oriented strategies that fit well with the prevailing climate of a culture that is preoccupied with success as the primary objective.

Unknowingly, we often reduce ministry into a cause-and-effect approach with immediate results as we overlook the long-term work that undergirds true spiritual formation. In this model, strategic planning and relevant programming are believed to be the key components that create transformation. As a result, we allow secondary strategies to eclipse a fundamental theological truth embedded in the scriptures: The kingdom of God is first and foremost a relational entity because God is relational.

In recent years, the doctrine of the Trinity, accompanied by a renewed emphasis on community, has surfaced in an attempt to push back the structures and values that allowed for private and independent spiritual journeys. The DNA of Trinitarian theology could never be repressed—we were made in the image of God. This return is directly related to an innate longing to recover the truth about the relational nature of God. The dynamic of Father, Son, and Holy Spirit in community from eternity past has been passed along to us. In his book, *The Great Dance*, C. Baxter Kruger writes: "The goal of the Trinity is inclusion. The purpose of the Father, Son and Spirit in creation is to draw us within their circle of shared life so that we too can experience it with them."[5]

When you look closely into literature written in the field of spiritual direction you discover how foundational the Trinitarian relationship truly is. William Barry, who has made a significant contribution says, "Thus, the ministry of spiritual direction helps individuals in the community to come to an ever deeper and more realistic conception of who God is in relationship to us."[6] Later he adds, "The aim of all ministry in the church, therefore, must be to make it more possible for us to pay attention to and carry out the deepest desire of our hearts, namely, to live in community with the Trinity and with one another."[7]

When we understand God's intentions for community at the deepest level, we begin to see the value of an intentional commitment to another person for the purpose of spiritual formation. To meet with a trusted spiritual director is to open oneself up to all the dynamics found in the inner world of our souls, a world that many of us are not only afraid to reveal to others, but are also unaware of ourselves. When we live independently of each other, we cut off the very pathway God intended for our growth. The Christian experience is not individualistic—it is nurtured in community. Barry suggests, "The model [for spiritual direction], of course, is the Triune God in whom the three Persons so completely share all they have and are with one another that they are One"[8]

In the ancient history of the church, this concept of God's interconnectedness was focused around the metaphor of dancing together. Barry highlights this unique perspective:

I am also reminded of the term the Greek Fathers used to describe the mutual dwelling of the three Persons of the Trinity, *perichoresis*, which some theologians interpret as meaning "dancing around." We have already noted how theologians say of the three persons that the only quality that distinguishes them from one another is their mutual relationships. To describe this mutuality of relationships, the dance is a lovely metaphor.[9]

In the minds of many leading thinkers within the Protestant tradition, this return to Trinitarian theology has become the theological undergirding for the ministry of spiritual direction. When we engage in this practice we "dance together" in the *perichoretic union* that opens us up to new discoveries of who God is and who we are. Such relationships of nurture were meant to be. The triune God calls us into spiritual friendships that allow us to probe our desires, temptations, joys, and sorrows with one another.

Since the metaphor of dance has entered the discussion, I will use it to make one more point. My wife coaxed me into dance lessons several years ago. This happened because my best friend's daughter was getting married and he was told to sign up for some lessons in preparation for the father-daughter dance at the reception. So there we were, two middle-aged guys stumbling around on the floor while an instructor tried to teach us the steps that led to graceful movement. How embarrassing! Clearly, I didn't know how to dance. It was foreign to my experience and my body was simply not oriented to this expression of refined foot stepping. I took consolation in the fact that my good friend was doing worse than I as we tried to learn the fox-trot, waltz, and swing.

Could it be that we don't know how to "dance" as soul friends anymore? Is it possible that the necessary moves to dance relationally have been lost? Could it be that most leaders have become conditioned to a style of management and programming that leaves no room for a Trinitarian philosophy of ministry? If Jesus showed up in today's Western culture, would he need to teach us how to dance? Might his first concern be the recovery of spiritual formation as a relational experience because we are created in the image of God who is Trinitarian in nature? We only need to look to his prayer for us to see the biblical foundation for relational spiritual formation: "My prayer is not for them alone. I pray also for those who will believe in me through their message, that all of them may be one, Father, just as you are in me and I am in you. May they also be in us so that the world may believe that you have sent me" (John 17:20–21).

I wonder what a kind of soul talk goes on among the members of the Trinity and how deeply the godhead desires his followers to rediscover this type of union and communion?

The Example of Christ

The intensely relational dynamic that characterizes the godhead becomes the centerpiece of Christ's life and ministry on earth. His relationality with the Father and the Holy Spirit undergirds and characterizes his practice of spiritual direction with others. Those who truly understand spiritual direction look to Christ's example as the strategic pattern from which we develop a philosophy of how to lead others. Margaret Guenther, in her book *Holy Listening*, writes, "The great model for all teachers, and certainly for all teachers who are spiritual directors, is Jesus himself."[10] Carolyn Gratton starts from the same place:

> If we really seek to understand something of the essence of spiritual direction, we need to pay attention to how Jesus himself went about it. He both reveals the directedness of all humanity toward intimacy with God and guides us into that relationship. We can begin by looking at the Gospels to see how he prepared for this

task. What major themes comprised the content of the direction he gave? How was he present to his directees? What in particular characterized the method of direction he used?[11]

Jesus' teaching style of spiritual guidance was not just oriented toward the masses in the context of his preaching. He spent a significant amount of time in personal dialogue with individuals. In the gospels, we discover that whenever a person sought Jesus out, they were received by him in a personal manner and given one-to-one time to process their spiritual journey. Jesus always began his discussion around the particulars of the individual's life circumstances and used these issues to lead each person to a deeper understanding of God's character, particularly his love. At the heart of spiritual direction is a commitment to this one-to-one concern for others.

In the life of Christ, we see this type of relational work taking place on a daily basis. He models soul friendship with his disciples by engaging in questions, discussing problems, assessing motives, and fostering awareness and growth. What takes place with the disciples could be called "group spiritual direction" (something we will examine more closely in chapter ten). Jesus always processed questions with questions. He asks his disciples to reflect and interpret significant experiences. He queries them on what they are thinking, feeling, and perceiving. Soul talk thrives in Jesus' world of relational encounters.

An incident in the life of the Apostle Peter represents a primary example of how spiritual direction takes place. In his book, *Soulguide*, Bruce Demarest[12] gives careful attention to the way in which Jesus processes Peter's denial and he highlights various aspects of effective spiritual direction:

1. *Jesus interceded for Peter* (Luke 22:32). A primary task of

any director is to be in prayer for those that he or she is leading. Christ is keenly attuned to Peter's temperament and prays for his protection and the development of his spiritual life amid the potential for failure.

2. *Jesus allowed Peter to experience failure.* It is easy for a director to attempt to protect an individual and, without knowing it, exercise control and foster false security. Good directors know that a valuable key in the journey of spiritual formation involves allowing the individual to face the truth about their inconsistency, false self, and the failures that will inevitably surface.

3. *Christ raised questions that forced Peter to look at his inner motives.* At the heart of effective spiritual direction is the art of asking questions—questions that lead the individual into a deeper understanding of their inner world and how this world shapes their outer responses. Throughout scripture Jesus asks profound questions. In John 21 he probes: "Peter, do you love me more than these?"

4. *Jesus strengthens Peter's hope in the midst of deep disappointment.* When the false self, weakness, and sin are brought to the surface, there is often a sense of despair in the life of the directee. At this point, a director can become the source whereby optimism is recovered. Certainly Peter is bordering on hopelessness following his betrayal. Yet, Christ reaffirms his calling and leads him out of his shame: "Feed my sheep."

Peter's relationship with Jesus is a wonderful example of effective spiritual direction. Jesus is the master of how to lead others into a deeper awareness of what God is seeking to do through all of the events that life brings.

In *Soulguide*, Bruce Demarest offers many other examples in the gospels where Christ models his commitment to the care of the soul. His visits with Martha and Mary must have been times when many questions brought personal concerns to the surface. On one occasion, we find Mary sitting at his feet. On that day, Martha is also brought into the formation process when Jesus queries her regarding the busyness of her life and the temptation to be distracted by secondary things. We know that Christ spent extended time in conversation with these women around their spiritual hunger and their journey toward an experiential knowledge of the Father.

In the gospels we find many other examples of one-to-one conversations with Christ. All of them offer insight into the art of spiritual direction. The story of the woman at the well (John 4:4–30) is a study in working with resistance, something very common to the process of spiritual direction. Resistance occurs when an individual seeks to avert an obvious issue of concern or apparent need. In the encounter with the woman, we see the value of Jesus' insightful questions as he helps to expose her shadow side and then nurture a pathway toward awareness and honesty. Spiritual directors need to discern resistance and gently help the individual to face his or her self-imposed spiritual roadblocks.

The story of the invalid at Bethesda (John 5:1–15) focuses on apathy. Once again, a probing question—"Do you want to get well?"—ignites an awareness of the need for new passion and desire in the man's life. In the context of spiritual direction we often have to help individuals face the fact that giving up a "sickness" will require courage and a whole new set of challenges.

The woman taken in adultery (John 8:1–22) portrays the importance of offering a safe place when someone is working through issues of moral failure. Spiritual direction provides the directee with a confidential setting to look at Jesus in the midst of intense failure and shame. The director models the relational compassion of Christ by creating a secure setting to process sin and find forgiveness.

The rich young ruler (Mark 10:17–22) exemplifies Christ's wisdom and discernment when it is necessary to bring to light those things that stand in the way of spiritual formation. There are times in spiritual direction when the guide needs to expose the false assumptions in a firm but compassionate manner. We are told "Jesus looked at him and loved him." It must have felt challenging to express the truth; yet Christ boldly pressed the issue.

Another example of Christ's relational commitment to spiritual formation would be his encounter with Zacchaeus (Luke 19:1–10). He extends his own invitation to dine with Zacchaeus in his home—a relational risk few would be willing to take! The decision to connect with this tax collector over a meal on his turf results in a life-altering experience!

At the heart of Christ's approach to spiritual development we discover a critical theme running through his interpersonal style. Jesus' focus is on fostering transformation by leading people into a new and deeper kind of seeing and hearing. Carolyn Gratton writes:

> Jesus Christ, the prototype of all spiritual directors, came with the message that people were to repent and change their lives because a new creation, a new world of meaning and value, his Kingdom, was at hand. . . . In the Gospels we see him revealing a fresh view of time, of human destiny, the meaning of history, the hidden directionality of the whole world and each person in it.[13]

This approach is central to Christ's strategy in helping people discover mystery, discern spiritual truth, and perceive the kingdom. Spiritual direction, in the truest sense, is a commitment to help the directee think intuitively as they seek to find the hand of God in places they might not otherwise look. The primary focus of the conversation is grounded in discerning where God is making himself present in our day-to-day journey.

The disciples on the road to Emmaus (Luke 24:13–32) demonstrate a wonderful example of how Christ invites us into this type of experiential encounter. After an extended time of walking and talking together, and then continued interaction over a meal, these disciples finally realize who this guest really is. They asked each other: "Were not our hearts burning within us while he talked with us on the road and opened the Scriptures to us?" (Luke 24:32).

Christ invites us to pay attention to the inner movements in our spirit as we process the everyday experiences of life to find his fingerprints. *He is not always evident, but he is always present. At the heart of spiritual direction is the assumption that we can discern his presence.*

Christ was always helping the seeker find God in the middle of the mundane, the painful and the confusing reality of their existence. The role of the director is simply to model Christ's example by guiding the directee to search for the evidence of God's loving purposes in all the events, experiences, and emotions that life brings.

The Example of Paul

The Apostle Paul offers many clues in his writings regarding the nature of spiritual direction. He functions as a "spiritual guide" to his "children."[14] To the Corinthians he wrote, "Even if you had ten thousand guardians in Christ, you do not have many fathers, for in Jesus Christ I became your father through the gospel. Therefore I urge you to imitate me" (1 Corinthians 4:15–16).

Timothy is the primary beneficiary of Paul's personal guidance. He refers to him as his "son" in 1 Corinthians 4:17. Later he says to him, "What you heard from me, keep as the pattern of sound teaching . . . guard the good deposit that was entrusted to you" (2 Timothy 1:13–14). And then, "You, however, know all about my teaching, my way of life" (2 Timothy 3:10).

In his epistles, Paul speaks of his "instruction" (1 Timothy 3:14) and his "example" (1 Corinthians 11:1). He offers a relational strategy for shaping the lives of those he disciples. To the Thessalonians he says, "Because we loved you so much, we were delighted to share with you not only the gospel of God but our lives as well. . . . For you know that we dealt with each of you as a father deals with his own children, encouraging, comforting and urging you to live lives worthy of God, who calls you into his kingdom and glory" (1 Thessalonians 2:8, 11–12).

Of course, while Paul was capable of offering a deep level of spiritual friendship to only a few, his endearing terms of affection reveal Paul's intention to be relationally involved with all his spiritual children. At the end of the Epistle to the Romans he offers a sizeable list of those people who have shared life and ministry together with him.

A primary text providing insight for those who offer spiritual direction to others is found in Galatians 4:19. Paul writes, "My dear children, for whom I am again in the pains of childbirth until Christ is formed in you." As we take a closer look at the phrases that make up this statement, we find Paul delineating the components he felt necessary in spiritual direction.

1. *"Dear children" – Spiritual direction is relational in nature.*

In recent years the church has found itself trapped in a highly structured, programmatic (and even mechanistic) approach as the faulty paradigm upon which we base and foster spiritual growth. Relational ministry (as exemplified by Christ and Paul) has given way to pragmatic, goal-oriented strategies.

Churches have reduced most things to a cause-and-effect structure, believing that information and programming are the keys to transformation. As a result, we have allowed secondary strategies to eclipse a fundamental theological truth embedded in the Word of

God—the kingdom is relational. Paul knows this and his writing breathes relationship, intimacy, compassion, and concern. The guidance he offers his close companions, and even those who cross his path briefly, comes from a deep passion to know and be known.

If we are to be involved in spiritual direction, there must be a sense of the parental concern that Paul shows. Leaders so easily see their colleagues and other individuals as a means to an end. Without realizing it, we participate in the "commodification of people"—we concern ourselves with what they can offer the organization (just a commodity) before we see them as image-bearers of God's nature. Spiritual direction recovers the relational nature of ministry—"my dear children."

2. *"The pains of childbirth" – Spiritual direction involves suffering.*

Paul understands that engaging in relational ministry will also involve pain. He is simply saying that, on this side of heaven, we will agonize with others in their spiritual journey. The fallenness of people greatly complicates the work of the leader—change does not come easily.

Paul is well aware of the hard work and, at times, the deep disillusionment that comes with relationships in ministry. Formation is all about suffering, not only for Paul, but also for the individuals he longs to see formed. Is not part of the leader's pain the vicarious angst he or she feels while watching others suffer through sickness, addictive behavior, broken relationships, and death? As we enter the desert of shared pain we find that God is able to do his greatest work.

Birthing a child is probably the most intimate metaphor Paul could use to describe the kind of work he was in and calls us to. At times, being a soul friend feels like being in spiritual birth labor. There are times when tears have streamed down my cheeks as I listened to the journey of another person. I ached as they wrestled to find hope.

3. *"Until Christ" – Spiritual direction is Christo-centric.*

Jesus Christ is the one and only person we call people to become like when we engage in the forming process. There are no other primary models, only secondary ones. In several places, Paul invites people to "follow me as I follow Christ."

The purpose of spiritual direction is to lead others to become attached to a Person—not a philosophy, a program, or a church. Karl Rahner, a Jesuit theologian, believes a "personal entering into this life of Jesus of Nazareth is a participation in the inner life of God; then the gaze into the face of Jesus of Nazareth is changed into the face-to-face vision of God."[15] Paul is passionate about creating a context where the individual encounters Christ in such deep and personal ways.

One of the great temptations in spiritual direction is to fail to see Christ in all things. In the end, everything matters and Christ is a part of each experience—the ecstatic and the mundane. Effective directors know how to stay Christo-centric. Without forcing the process, their goal is to help the directee find Christ in each and every aspect of life.

4. *"Formed in you" – Spiritual direction is process oriented.*

The word "formed" is rich with meaning in the scriptures, coming from the Greek word *morphoo*, from which we get our word "morph." "*Morphoo* means 'the inward and real transformation of the essential nature of a person.' It was the term used to describe the formation and growth of an embryo in a mother's body."[16] At the heart of Pauline spiritual formation is the concept of "forming"— he is committed to intentional work in the lives of individuals with a view to transformation over their entire journey.

Central to spiritual direction is the belief that growth is occurring; spiritual life is being formed, but only as we take the time necessary to work at it together. When Paul talks about Christ being formed in us he knows it involves relationships plus time. In our program-centric approach to ministry we have lost our grip on the necessity of time in the process of transformation. If we hope to see Christ formed in others, we have to be willing to stay in it over the long haul.

The realization that spiritual "morphing" involves relationships plus time recently hit home in my life. I received a long distance call from a man (now in his late 40s) who was a teenager when I led Youth for Christ. Tim was kind of an odd guy, always looking for the fun and never seeming to take things seriously. I never really saw much change in his life as a teenager. But the commitment to relational ministry was a core value in Youth for Christ. So we hung in there.

Thirty years have passed since I said good-bye to Tim. He graduated and we left the city. I would never have expected to hear from him again. Apparently, he found me through the SoulFormation website on the internet and then called.

"Are you Morris Dirks—the guy who used to lead Youth for Christ?" I confirmed that he found the right person. He said, "I'm Tim—do you remember me?" I told him that I did. And then came these words that took me by surprise: "I am with some men and we are thinking back to the people who had significant impact on our lives. I just want you to know that I would never have made it through high school without you." I was stunned . . . Christ was "morphing" Tim all along. Relationships plus time lead to spiritual transformation.

Paul has offered one short verse: "My dear children, for whom I am again in the pains of childbirth until Christ is formed in you" (Galatians 4:19). In this text we have a wealth of implications to process when it comes to the importance of soul friendships with others.

The Self-Revealing Nature of God

There is one more aspect that must be explored if we desire to ground the ministry of spiritual direction biblically and theologically. This fundamental truth is the self-revealing nature of God. At the heart of directing others is the intention to help them discern where and how God is revealing himself. (Later, we will discover this as a primary theme in Ignatian spirituality—"finding God in all things.")

William Reiser, in his book appropriately titled *Seeking God in All Things: Theology and Spiritual Direction*, believes that direction rests upon a theology of revelation:

Direction presumes that God continues to communicate the divine presence and life to human beings who are constantly being formed or created in ways not significantly different from the classic accounts of God's speaking to women and men that we find in Scripture. . . . [R]evelation, when understood as God's self-communication, is always happening.[17]

This concept of "self-communication" is observable when Jesus says to Peter, "Blessed are you, Simon son of Jonah, for this was not revealed to you by flesh and blood, but by my Father in heaven" (Matthew 16:17). Then, when Paul prays for the Ephesians he says, "I pray that the eyes of your heart may be enlightened" (Ephesians 1:18). The dominant leaders and writers of the New Testament agree that the center of the Christian life is to be experiential in nature. It is all about God's revelation of himself to the believer.

Yet, we also know, according to the scriptures, that it isn't easy to find God in all things. He comes to us in hidden and often counterintuitive ways. As I noted earlier, "God comes to you disguised as your life." One of the challenges is to find him amid the busyness, the routine, the pain, and the confusion that so easily overshadows the mystery of God in the world. In response to this tendency toward a mindless existence—one that is disconnected from spiritual reality—we find the need for ongoing support to keep looking, seeking, and pursuing an inner experience, a personal awareness, of God. Francis Vanderwall states:

> This is why we seek spiritual direction—because deep down inside us, unspoken perhaps, but nevertheless experienced, we know that there is more, much more, than the superficiality of the daily grind, and we long for the depths of our beings to be evoked so that the deep within us may be united to the deep of God.[18]

Because this desire for God is innate, we hunger for help in discerning how God is revealing himself amid life's circumstances. Spiritual direction offers the kind of relationship where those longings and questions can be explored. Maureen Conroy contends, "God is a self-communicating God who reveals self through creation, Scripture, life experience, human relationships, solitude and prayer. . . . In other words, God can be experienced in hearts, minds, imaginations, psyches, and bodies."[19]

The focus of spiritual direction, then, is this self-revealing heart of God. It can be described as "help given by one Christian to another, which enables that person to pay attention to God's personal communication to him or her, to respond to this personally communicating God, and to live out the consequences of this relationship."[20] Such help is critical if we hope to guide others into avenues of knowing God, avenues that might remain closed without the wisdom of an outside voice.

For too long the Christian church has failed to embrace the self-revealing nature of God. We have feared experiential spirituality and the concept that God reveals anything outside of that which has been given in the written Word. Yet, when the apostles speak of "knowing" God, they are moving beyond intellectual understanding (something assumed within the Greek culture) toward the Hebrew concept, which is relational. A closer look at the biblical texts[21] will reveal an obvious invitation to "know" the self-communicating God experientially.

New Testament scholars would agree that to "have genuine knowledge one must respond to God who has graciously made himself known.... Knowing God, therefore, is more than theoretical or intellectual knowledge."[22] This experiential knowledge, which is at the center of New Testament Christianity, is also at the heart of spiritual direction.

In conclusion, it becomes obvious that there are many avenues that converge on the basic assumption that the practice of spiritual direction is Christo-centric and thoroughly biblical. A close look at the scriptures, and the nature of Christian experience confirmed therein, would substantiate the assumption that we were made to encounter God at a personal and existential level.

Additionally, the scriptures verify that this journey toward God is cultivated best when we intentionally open our world up to other people—soul friends or spiritual guides—who help one another to discern the work of God in and around us.

A Spiritual Direction Story
Todd Gorton – A Pastor

Nine years ago my career was booming. In ministry-speak, I would say God was leading me to new and unique opportunities to serve him more broadly. I had just accepted a leadership position across the country in a high profile mega-church and was thrilled with my newfound confidence; opportunities were in abundance.

Within a year I was beginning to run down, so logically I ramped up my responsibilities and began to toy around with the idea of an even bigger leadership role. At the same time, by the grace of God, I began to enter into what would become a relationship with my spiritual director.

Shortly thereafter I began to realize that I was suffering from spiritual apathy. I thought making a change would satisfy, so I bolstered my ministry résumé. This led to another cross-country move for our family as I sought out a new pastoral role in a rapidly changing church.

Looking back, it was a spiritual director that saved my life . . . well, at least my ministry and quite possibly my attitude. Since my first awkward conversations, to the deep joining of two people and the power of the Holy Spirit, the relationship has functioned as a type of life-saving and life-giving spiritual tether. Spiritual direction has quite literally kept me grounded.

Close to where we live is a huge park. In the park is a giant balloon. This balloon is very unique. It is one of the largest helium balloons in the United States at 118 feet tall with a gondola that carries up to thirty passengers. The balloon itself holds 210,000 cubic feet of helium and remains tethered to the ground by a steel cable with the breaking strength of over 90,000 pounds.

In my life, spiritual direction plays the same role as that steel cable. It is a tether. My spiritual director reminds me who God is while helping me remember who I am supposed to be. As we have our times of direction together we discuss, pray, and engage the Holy Spirit.

For me spiritual direction simply involves seeking God together with an older and wiser man who loves Jesus, loves me, and has a deep understanding of how God works. I've known my spiritual director now for many years. As we live in different states, we have our times of direction together over the phone. It is still very effective.

Today I serve a local community church of about 2,000 adults, where the daily pressures of pastoring and leading abound. However, I continue to strip away my false assumptions of God and how I relate to Jesus. Each month my spiritual director assists as a guide to foster my seeking. Together we search for a day-to-day connection with God that is fresh and new.

As I continue choosing to be tethered through the act and art of spiritual direction, I'm finding what it is to be loved and to deeply love, what it looks like to fail and succeed and how to live in the extraordinary ordinary of each day.

5

Going Back Before We Go Forward:
Saint Ignatius and the Spiritual Exercises

And now, I must introduce you to someone special. I suppose most of us have a favorite leader in the history of the church—a "patron saint." If we were on a retreat together it would be fun to go around the circle to hear which spiritual leader you would pick from the past 2,000 years.

I'm going with Ignatius of Loyola (1491–1556). Here's why: Ignatius demonstrated the kind of guidance that is desperately needed in today's church. He enlisted hundreds of leaders in a Christo-centric missionary movement, a call to activism that impacted the continent of Europe. *At the same time he fostered a contemplative foundation for this activism—an experiential relationship with Christ as the starting point for their work.* While Martin Luther was igniting the Protestant Reformation, Ignatius was working diligently on the other side of the fence forging a "counter-reformation," a spiritual renewal movement within the Roman Catholic Church. A careful study of his life reveals that he does not belong to one religious side or the other—his life is bigger than that. It is a display of transformational leadership that offers profound lessons for us in today's world.

We often talk about "being and doing" in a way that implies

most people in ministry struggle to balance exterior activism with times of solitude and interior reflection. We search for examples to help us find the pathway that knits both together. Of course, Jesus perfectly displays this equilibrium. Ignatius studied the life of Christ so carefully that he was able to model the mysterious balance that exemplifies healthy leadership. Ignatius mastered being and doing in such a way that he is often referred to as a *contemplative in action.*

I'm going with Ignatius for a second reason. He modeled and taught us how to practice spiritual direction better than any other leader in the history of the church. If we desire to learn more about forming the leader's soul, Ignatius is a towering example for us to study. For that reason, I will spend several chapters of this book processing the key principles passed on to us by this man who gave himself to understanding, practicing, and training others in the art of spiritual direction. Before we do, it will be helpful to highlight the impact Ignatius exerted on spiritual formation and direction for the past five hundred years.

A Contemplative in Action

Ignatius gave birth to the Society of Jesus (Jesuits). When he died, there were 1,000 missionaries spread out over Europe. These spiritual pioneers had experienced something many leaders lack today: Ignatius had shaped the spiritual horizon of their inner world and not just their ministry careers. He truly could say, "Follow me as I follow Christ." He did this by developing a paradigm of spiritual direction that was Christo-centric and transformational, a model that has continued to influence leaders to this day. Furthermore, his guiding principles have gained momentum in recent decades, and many authors in the field of spiritual formation are now drawing from the discoveries and practices that are rooted in Ignatius.

Ignatius stands out on the landscape of Christian history

as one who believed the practice of spiritual direction was so significant that it was worth giving much of his life to. His dream was that others would treasure his discoveries and apply them to their spiritual walk. What he discerned for himself, and then wrote for others, is still published and practiced today: *The Spiritual Exercises of Saint Ignatius.*

We discover that as a contemplative in action, Ignatius was a person who understood the nature of spiritual leadership at the deepest level. His balance of being and doing has particular relevance to Christian leaders in today's context of ministry. We live in a world of action, and yet we are called to engage in an experiential union with Christ amid the busyness of leading others. The doing side almost always wins! In fact, there are those who pit the contemplative against the activist and fail to see that the two are not opposites but rather counterparts to each other. In today's world of busy Christian leadership, we need contemplatives in action, leaders who know how to guide us to emotional and spiritual health amid the demands of ministry.

It is my contention that the current resurgence of interest in spiritual formation in ministry is directly related to the realization that activism without contemplation results in leaders who are spiritually diseased. Loss of calling, disillusionment, stress, anxiety, and burnout are directly connected to the success models that are showcased and coveted by leaders who develop idolatrous careers of ministry accomplishment while neglecting the soul. Jesus' question rebounds into our lives when he asks, "What good is it for someone to gain the whole world, and yet lose or forfeit their very self [their soul]?" (Luke 9:25).

Certainly we see the souls of leaders strewn along the highway of ministry advancement. Having neglected their interior life, they were seduced into thinking that doing is being. We have discovered the painful truth—such a way of life does not lead to sustainable ministry.

Ignatius stands out as someone who knew how to balance the demands of ministry while practicing a relational union with Christ. He led the way in helping us understand the pathway to full engagement in ministry while developing a lifestyle of contemplative mysticism. It was Ignatius' desire that his discoveries of how to walk with Christ amid the demands of ministry would be passed on to other leaders. Maureen Conroy describes his dedication to the spiritual formation of others:

> Ignatius of Loyola, a spiritual director who has inspired many spiritual directors during the past four centuries . . . helped individuals open themselves to experience God in a personal way. Then he helped them to recognize, understand, and respond to their experience and to see the difference in themselves as a result of God's touch. He did this so well for others because he did it so well within himself.[1]

With painstaking effort, Ignatius carefully processed the spiritual discoveries he made in his own life and then sought to make a record of them for others. These insights, once gathered, refined, and expanded over the years, became known as the *Spiritual Exercises*. Ignatius worked hard to understand the common dynamics related to spiritual growth. His goal was to find the pathway whereby people could engage in an intimate relationship with God by perceiving the various movements that occurred in their inner being and to process these with God at an experiential level.

If we are seeking to develop a model of spiritual direction for Christian leaders in today's world, we must turn to Ignatius as a primary contributor to this field. His wisdom and practical strategy for spiritual formation continue to be a leading source to train others who desire to serve as spiritual guides. Philip Sheldrake, a

British Jesuit and co-director of the Institute of Spirituality writes:

> Ignatius's vision was that the *Spiritual Exercises* and the spirituality which came from it could only be transmitted in a vital way from person to person, for he saw the *Exercises* as an experience rather than a collection of maxims. Thus, Ignatius sought to form people who would *live* the *Exercises* until their minds were simply reflections of the spirit.[2]

Sheldrake also notes, "Many people, nowadays, experience the *Spiritual Exercises* as a highly effective instrument for spiritual growth. For some, exposure to the *Exercises* has been akin to a conversion experience."[3] The rediscovery of Ignatius and his spiritual teachings is a bright spot for those who desire a deeper union with Christ.

A Brief History of St. Ignatius

Ignatius was born near the small town of Azpeitia in Castle Loyola, which was located in the Basque country of northern Spain. His original name was *Iñigo*, but while in Paris, it became *Ignatius*, a name more familiar to non-Spaniards. He was born in 1491 during the reformation era and became a catalyst of renewal within the Roman Catholic tradition. In John Donnelly's history of Ignatius, he contends: "Arguably, Ignatius of Loyola contributed more than anyone to reforming and refashioning Catholicism."[4]

As a young man, Ignatius was a page of the royal treasurer in Spain, and he accompanied his master on journeys throughout the country. At this time, he had no spiritual passion—other ambitions dominated his horizon—as he was preoccupied with the life of a gallant and elegant courtier. He was frequently involved in duels, brawls, and fights. When he was not furthering his career ambitions as a soldier, he dedicated himself to womanizing and gambling.

Until the age of thirty, Ignatius was a man who shamelessly gave himself to the vanities of the world with an intense love of the martial exercises and a greedy commitment to winning fame among his peers. In time, he took up arms as a soldier against the French who laid siege to the Spanish fortification of Pamplona in May of 1521. Though he found himself in a losing battle, he refused to surrender and paid dearly when he was seriously wounded by a small cannonball that smashed his right leg. It was this personal catastrophe that became the means whereby God reordered his life.

After the doctors set his bones, Ignatius' health declined, leading to confinement for nine months of convalescence back home in Loyola. During this time of isolation, the only books available were religious in nature, and it was this literature that resulted in Ignatius' conversion to Christ and a transformed life. He became a new kind of soldier. Ignatius had always dreamed of recognition for his heroic deeds by an earthly king, but now he caught a vision of serving God as king of kings. Paul Doncoeur writes:

> For his prince he had thrown himself, at the risk of his life, into the thick of the battle. He fell fighting bravely, only to find himself illuminated by a splendor far brighter than any military glory. He arose a prouder champion in the service of a nobler Master.[5]

Following his conversion, Ignatius left for a monastery in Montserrat, Spain, where he ultimately made his first confession that, according to tradition, took all of three days. Shortly thereafter, he moved to Manresa, about a five-hour journey, where he gave his nobleman's clothes to a beggar, and in the months to follow, Ignatius lived in solitude. He chose to enter his own personal wilderness, one that exposed him "to the extremes of his own personality, as well as the depths of God's love. There in his cave, he experiences the very best of himself and the very worst. The worst leaves him close to suicide. The best leaves him close to God."[6]

During this wilderness season, an encounter with Christ took place that was experiential and transformational. Later, as Ignatius told his friends about what had happened during this time of isolation and spiritual searching, he said, "God treated him at this time just as a schoolmaster treats a child whom he is teaching."[7] Karl Rahner writes of Ignatius' life-changing experience with Christ:

> Everything he had ever learnt in his whole life seemed insignificant in comparison. He felt he had become a new and changed man. . . . He saw Jesus Christ from now on as the gentle king and lord who came to fulfill the spread of the kingdom of God which had dawned. Iñigo sensed his vocation to become a worker with and for Christ. . . . The essential basic insights of his mystical experience he put down in writing in his book of *Spiritual Exercises*.[8]

The *Exercises* ultimately became a book of personalized spiritual direction and practices born out of Ignatius' experiences and his deep hunger to know Christ. Regarding these personal discoveries, he says, "The scales were lifted from my spiritual eyes and everything could be seen in God himself. This was the experience I longed to communicate to others through the exercises I offered them."[9] At the center of the *Exercises* is the conviction that there are movements in the heart that lead either toward God or away from him. It is important to understand this aspect of Ignatian spirituality as it undergirds everything else. Margaret Silf states:

> His own moods—reflectors of those hidden inner movements, the God-focused joy and the self-focused despair—help him to find his way forward, by trial and error, on his inner journey to God. He learns how to use his feelings and reactions, and his memories and desires, as pointers to help him seek out what, in every situation,

is leading him closer to God and to leave aside anything that is causing him to drift away from God.[10]

Following his transformative experience in Manresa, Ignatius set off for Paris to begin his education and the dream of ordination in the Catholic Church. This began an extended period of travel and further education. Each chapter in this stage of his life involved a deepening of his obedience and love for Christ, leading to deeper prayer and action. Throughout his life and travels, Ignatius developed significant relationships (soul friends) with people who shared his passion to know Christ and serve him with abandon. The companions of Ignatius not only studied and practiced the *Spiritual Exercises*, they also joined together in a common mission and made a decision to bind themselves to religious vows, which became the foundation for The Society of Jesus (later to be known as the Jesuit Religious Order).[11]

In time, Ignatius traveled to Rome, seeking the blessing of the Pope. On the way to Rome, Ignatius had a mystical experience of Christ and heard these words: "I will be favorable to you in Rome." He also saw Christ carrying his cross and the Father saying to his Son, "I want you to take this man as your servant." Christ then said to Ignatius, "I desire you to serve us."[12] In 1540, when Ignatius was forty-nine years old, Pope Paul III officially approved the Society of Jesus as a religious order.

What followed over the next sixteen years was worldwide influence by Ignatius and his companions. As a "contemplative in action" he forged a movement that crisscrossed Europe and spread overseas. When Ignatius died on July 31, 1556, there were approximately 1,000 Jesuits in the religious order serving in seventeen communities. His life was one of transformational spirituality that resulted in a strategy of influence that crossed all borders.

Ignatius' spiritual authenticity as a leader dates back to his extended experience of solitude in Manresa (1522). There he processed how one walks in personal intimacy with Christ. The exercises, when shared with others, seemed unusually valuable to all who desired true union with Christ. They became the foundation upon which Ignatius gathered companions and led them into a life of contemplation and action. During his life, he continued to refine these exercises; it was not until 1540, almost twenty years after he had first begun to write down his thoughts, that Ignatius put the final touches on the sheaf of notes that would become the *Spiritual Exercises*. This practical wisdom has since been studied throughout the centuries by sincere seekers of Christ.

It has been said, "Ignatius had a heart big enough to hold the universe."[13] This heart continues to influence serious Christ-followers today. Margot Patterson expresses the ongoing impact of his life as follows: "The *Spiritual Exercises* of St. Ignatius are being turned to by growing numbers of people who say the 450-year-old primer on prayer and contemplation offers a personal encounter with the divine."[14]

Encountering God's Love

The *Exercises* are directional. By this, I mean they are oriented around what Ignatius called the *four weeks* designed to build on one another. The progression moves from conversion on the front end to fully devoted service in the kingdom of God at the conclusion. While they are called "weeks," Ignatius was more concerned that a transformational experience took place before the participant moved on. *Week one* was foundational. *Ignatius believed a radical encounter with the unconditional love of God was necessary before any forward movement into a life of discipleship could occur.*

To experience this intense embrace of God's grace, Ignatius maintained that a person must fully grasp the gravity of their sinfulness. His goal was to expose us to the desperate reality of our condition in such a way that we see only one possibility for recovery—grace. Ignatius intends to hold you over the very precipice of hell so that you can discover the unconditional wonder of what God has done for you through Christ.

When you read the *Exercises* you might find Ignatius' attempts to help you imagine the severity of your lost condition as somewhat *old fashioned* and unnecessary. Not so! He simply believes that you cannot appreciate the Good News until you have understood the bad news. Grace is only as meaningful as the situation from which we were rescued; Ignatius is determined to help a person embrace the depths of grace so that God's love is experienced as overwhelming. It is from this foundational experience that he believes we are aligned with God for all that follows.

If you read the *Exercises* you will note that they are recorded in the form of "annotations"—370 in all. The *Exercises* read as a somewhat complex and rather detailed manual. For this reason, those who are exploring them for the first time would be wise to use a contemporary translation allowing for easier understanding. (I would recommend the translation by David L. Fleming, *Draw Me into Your Friendship: A Literal Translation and a Contemporary Reading of the Spiritual Exercises.*) For the purpose of this study, over the next few chapters we will draw out the relevant themes that permeate the *Exercises* and offer invaluable insights into the process of spiritual direction.

However, before we move onto themes of spiritual formation, we must agree with Ignatius that everything will be off center unless grace is in place. *Right action flows out of a deep-seated sense of wonder that we have entered into an undeserved realm of unconditional love.* It is this radical embrace of grace that fills life with wonder and awe and calls us forward into a life of service. Effective spiritual direction begins where Ignatius began, by inviting the directee to experience grace at every point along the way!

A Spiritual Direction Story
Paul Rhoads – Associate Director, SoulFormation (Former Executive Director, Church Resource Ministries)

I didn't discover the sphere of spiritual formation and the discipline of spiritual direction until I had been a pastor for more than fifteen years. I was just about to move from southern California to the Pacific Northwest and from pastoral ministry to a leadership role in a parachurch ministry. I can remember praying that God would lead me to a spiritual director, but I thought it would be years before I found one (I only knew one person in the Northwest). Within one year I connected to a well-qualified and experienced spiritual director. It turns out my spiritual director was a former Jesuit priest who was well schooled in Ignatian spirituality. I learned many things during those first years, but two memories stand out.

The first memory goes back to my initial spiritual direction appointments. After greeting me and briefly connecting, my director paused—and then asked this very simple question, "So, how is your soul today?" I remember the power with which that simple question struck me. I had never been asked that before. Many caring friends and mentors had over the years asked how I was doing, but no one had asked how my soul was. I soon realized I didn't know how to answer that question. I had engaged in healing therapy with an excellent Christian counselor, so I knew how to describe my feelings and internal struggles. But I did not know how to articulate the state of my soul or the state of my relationship with God. I stumbled at first. My director helped me with more questions, but over time I learned how to answer that question and talk with clarity about my relationship with Jesus.

My second memory came in the middle of another session. I was wondering whether I really loved God very much, whether I was passionate about what was important to God. I could only see my failures, my shortcomings, my bent desires. With kindness and grace my director replied with a simple observation that validated the work God had been doing for years. He simply said, "Oh, I have no doubt about your desire and longing for God. It comes up every session. I simply have to touch it with a word and it spills over in intense emotion and tears. God has planted a strong desire for himself in you!"

Currently I am engaged in group spiritual direction for the first time. To be honest, I was skeptical when we started this journey. After two excellent spiritual directors, I wondered how significant this would be. The three of us are colleagues so that both enhances and creates challenges. We are all learners when it comes to group spiritual direction.

Recently I brought a discernment issue to the group regarding a possible ministry trip to Europe. Prior to the meeting I was convinced I should go. However, during our session God surfaced issues in me that were impinging on the decision and clouding my perspective. Our meeting provided enough clarity that, within a few days, our work as a group provided the insight I needed to make a firm decision. . . . I chose to stay home.

When we meet, each person is given time to present a topic related to his or her walk with God. Something significant happens. New clarity emerges; new insight is gained; the Spirit's voice is discerned with more conviction. There have been moments where one of us received just enough to take the next step. But we have also experienced break-through moments when something changed inside, something was released, where healing occurred.

It's been one year since our triad embarked on this journey together. I now look forward to group direction as much as I did individual spiritual direction. The further we go the more I realize the hidden potential of this transformational approach to spiritual formation.

6

Motives Matter:
Attached to the Wrong Thing

In this chapter, we are going to look at a primary theme that the Ignatian model offers contemporary leaders—one that is central to the *Spiritual Exercises*. Ignatius believed freedom was possible only as one was able to address what he called "inordinate attachments" or "disordered affections" that target the well-being of one's soul. This is soul-work at the level of our motivations. When it comes to spiritual formation in our own lives, and the lives of those to whom we offer spiritual direction, it is critical to understand this component as it undergirds all forward movement in the spiritual life, particularly in the lives of those who lead Christian organizations.

Ignatius succinctly states the primary intent of the *Exercises*: The purpose is to help the leader "to conquer himself, and to regulate his life so that he will not be influenced in his decisions by any inordinate attachment."[1] Ignatius desired to call forth committed disciples who aspired to realize an experiential union with Christ, one in which inordinate attachments or disordered affections were carefully tracked and processed. This is the fundamental assumption of Ignatius: Everything is to be surrendered to a higher purpose, and, in so doing, the individual moves onto a pathway of spiritual and emotional health. Søren Kierkegaard captures this same thought so well in the title of his book: *Purity of Heart is to*

Will One Thing. Ignatius is concerned about the "one thing" and offers practical help in guiding us there!

John English, in his book *Spiritual Freedom* writes, "Disordered attachments turn us in on ourselves; they are strictly concerned with self. . . . Ignatius speaks, then, about disordered attachments because they are enslaving. They chain us and prevent us from being free."[2] He believed that God wants our happiness and fulfillment as his primary objective; however, abandonment to his purposes is the only way to reach this goal.

If we are honest with ourselves we will uncover distorted intentions in many areas of life as we take on the challenge to "will one thing." For the purposes of this book, I would like to focus on twisted motives in ministry. In recent years I have come to believe that all kinds of inordinate attachments are seeded into the soil of ministry; many of them are presented as honorable attributes modeled by many spiritually heroic leaders. Yet, lurking behind these glittering accomplishments is the dangerous tendency to fill a hole that only Christ is sufficient for. I would like to take the Ignatian concept of inordinate attachments and process three motivations that derail the leader. These *attachments* often drive leaders into dangerous places, yet they go unnoticed and are often praised. They are the hidden saboteurs of the spiritual and emotional health that God intended for his leaders.

How did this happen? Somewhere, early on in life we developed what is called a "false self," also referred to as an "adaptive self." We were meant for a world of perfect love, security, and union with God. This ideal was lost in the garden. The false self began when Adam and Eve covered themselves to hide their shame. They were no longer properly aligned with the indwelling image of God. Fear became the driving emotion. Perfect love was sabotaged in their souls, and they believed the only form of self-protection was to adopt a new way of being.

We continue to find ourselves in the same dilemma. The false self creates artificial security and opens the door to motivational structures that rely on a human strategy for survival rather than trusting in God. By developing a survival project—one that is not centered on God's unconditional love—we take control and our tactics become self-focused. We unknowingly develop this false way of being as we attempt to become the managers of our own lives. Because our world has fallen into sin and ruin, we rely on this self-management plan, believing it will protect us from the brokenness we see and feel. However, this attempt to maintain control is precisely where the brokenness continues.

All of this is especially evident in ministry, which takes on hazardous characteristics when this false self becomes unknowingly entangled in our leadership style. We become laced with intentions and ideals that seem to be good—they might even appear to be "religious"—but actually serve self and not God. Because our adaptive strategies follow us into ministry, we need to make a concerted effort to discover where we have moved God to the sidelines in favor of our seemingly good intentions.

At first, our faulty approach to leadership appears to work, but in the end it backfires on us and on others. Sooner or later, we find ourselves hitting the wall; yet our false motivations run so deep we are unable to locate the reason for our pain and disillusionment. We press ahead as our inordinate attachments remain unchecked. If we hope to gain freedom, we will have to do some inner work. Ignatius leads us there. He invites us to process the shadows that distort our motivations at a fundamental level. We are ready to zero in on three motivations where we find the false self is secretly at work in the leader's life.[3]

Inordinate Attachment #1:

The Need to Be Liked – Working to Keep Others Happy

At the core of their being, people with this type of motivation have a deep need to be needed. They spend a significant amount of emotional energy wondering about what others are thinking and what they need to do to please them. This is classic codependent behavior: "What do I have to do to make you happy so that I can be happy?"

In the ministry we have a perfect setup for people who are given to pleasing others. There is no end to the opportunities we can find when it comes to doing things to make other people's lives easier or happier. However, for this person, the motivation for caring and leading others is easily tainted; it is self-focused. Behind the pleaser's ministry actions is a well-disguised hook, a strategy to get something in return. The return is affirmation, affection, praise, and encouragement.

People who are motivated by the need to be liked are extremely tuned in to the emotions of others. It is as if they have special antennae to detect the moods, responses, and feelings of those who matter in their world. At this point, they adapt their behavior to suit the feelings of the other person and begin to function in ways that bring the desired outcome—love and affirmation. This style of motivation involves a loss of identity. The leader's poor boundaries, and a lack of self-differentiation, result in an obsession—pleasing people becomes the primary pathway to maintain influence; however, in the end, this motivation is guaranteed to lead to emotional exhaustion.

Ignatius would seek to help this individual address their inordinate attachment to please and be praised. The transformational goal is for God to expose the fears that drive the codependent's leadership style. Sooner or later, this individual needs to come to a place where they are able to listen to God before listening to others.

They must come to understand who they are in Christ over and above who they are in the eyes of others. When this happens, they are free of the inordinate attachment that has sabotaged their soul. No longer do they live chained to an obsessive and manipulative strategy to be loved by others as the driving focus for their sense of worth.

The introduction to this book began with my confession to a psychiatrist: "I have totally and completely lost my way." On the day I entered his office, all I knew was that anxiety and depression were overwhelming me. I wanted out—give me the right pill so I can be happy again! However, long-term healing came in a different package. I had to find my way to the inordinate attachment—the obsessive and compulsive energy that was undermining my emotional well-being and my ability to know God's unconditional love.

At that point I began to see a spiritual director, and we processed the questions that were behind the difficult emotions in my soul. I discovered something that had escaped me for more than forty-five years. I was codependent, I was a pleaser—and my primary drug of choice was affirmation from the people who appreciated the way I functioned. I also came to realize how sin was at the core of this twisted motivation. Once that realization surfaced, I felt a deep sorrow for the way I had made ministry about me and not God. I entered an extended season of repentance. It felt right to grieve, and what followed was joy and freedom.

Christian ministry seems so worthy; yet we must be aware that it offers us a seductively powerful environment where we easily become trapped in cycles of behavior that undermine spiritual, emotional, and even physical health. People who enter helping professions (such as ministry) are naturally given to love and care for others. However, alongside of this strength there is often a weakness—the need to be needed. Sometimes we love others because we want to be loved.

In the end, the need to please and be liked was my disordered affection and, I must say, it caused a great deal of pain when God lovingly but firmly revealed my twisted motives. It wasn't until I was forced into a season of honest self-reflection that I was finally able to get in touch with what my anxiety and depression were truly saying. My life was speaking. I am grateful for a spiritual guide who helped me listen to what was being said.

Inordinate Attachment #2:
The Need to Succeed – Working to Win Others' Approval

Unlike the first type, this leader is more concerned about the project than they are about people. Task—not relationships—takes over as the obsessing focus. The primary goal is accomplishment. Of course, behind this is a deep need for approval, but the approval is directly linked to succeeding. Leaders who are controlled by the need to succeed have one primary fear: failure.

At the heart of this motivational style is an assumption; the leader stakes everything on a positive outcome. "I must succeed to be valuable or worthwhile." Somewhere along the way, this type of leader came to believe that who you are (your identity) is tied to what you do, and how well you do it. As a result, career performance became the singular place where they gained a sense of worth. When David McQueen, a success-driven pastor, woke up to his inordinate attachment, he wrote:

> And then one day it hit me. God was neither in my goals nor my means. Deep down, the reason I was leading a church and the reason I wanted to grow it was for me— for me to feel successful, for me to feel significant, for me to receive glory. Through several events, I felt God teaching me a foundational lesson: this isn't about you, and you can't do this thing called church without me.[4]

In the ministry world, a leader's inordinate attachment to success can run wild since the church is an organization that aspires to grow. As a result, programs, events, buildings, budgets, staff, and all other types of measurable outcomes become the focus. As the late Dallas Willard has said, "The greatest threat to devotion to Christ is service for Christ."[5] Successful ministry becomes the idolatrous master of this leader.

Sadly, such workaholism is often rewarded by the church or organization since it is regarded as the sincere sacrifice of a leader who truly desires God's kingdom to advance. In our culture of consumer Christianity, people will take any success you offer as another place to enjoy the good life.

A leader whose identity is not secure in Christ is easy prey for the false motivations that are linked to success as the primary motivation. It's tragic when a leader uses the church or organization he or she leads as the place to secure his or her sense of value and significance. Everyone under such a leader's influence is actually being played out as a means to the award that has become an obsession. Success means accomplishment and the praise that follows.

Often, the successful leader will need to hit the wall before they are able to wake up to the inordinate attachment that obsesses them. Their greatest fear—failure—might actually become a self-fulfilling prophecy as the leader over-performs in an attempt to reach their dream. Ignatius would call us to the freedom that is possible only when this type of leader finally discovers their ulterior motive and is able to serve God, having been freed from a self-made agenda. When this happens, the leader is capable of listening to God as he or she steps back from the addictive passions that sabotaged their true calling. They shift from a compulsive way of viewing life and ministry into a contemplative pattern— one where they are able to slow down, reflect, and hear the voice of God amid the many voices calling for successful outcomes.

In recent decades, the church-growth movement set the stage for what became the "attractional church model," an approach to church leadership that magnified the obsession with success. In fact, the fixation with growth and measurable outcomes fostered the idolatrous nature of this inordinate attachment. Without realizing it, the pursuit of successful ministries became more important than relational union with God and transformed lives.

If we receive spiritual direction, or offer it to other leaders, it is important to realize that our culture has bought into a myth: "to lead is to succeed." This is the internal message, and the lie, that constantly captures us as we seek to oversee ministry organizations. It takes great courage to refuse this seductive assumption as it infects our ministry mindset, either consciously or subconsciously. Effective spiritual direction is the place where we can take positive steps to dismantle this faulty foundation.

Viktor Frankl, the Viennese psychiatrist who experienced the horror of the holocaust, wrote a book describing his experience in World War II concentration camps. To his surprise, the book sold more than two million copies. In response to such success, Frankl writes the following in his introduction:

> I admonish my students both in Europe and America: "Don't aim at success—the more you aim at it and make it the target, the more you are going to miss it. For success, like happiness, cannot be pursued; it must ensue, and it only does so as the unintended side-effect of one's personal dedication to a cause greater than oneself . . . you have to let it [success] happen by not caring about it. I want you to listen to what your conscience commands you to do and go on to carry it out to the best of your knowledge. Then you will live to see that in the long run, I say!—success will follow you precisely because you had *forgotten* to think about it."[6]

Frankl is touching down on the very truth that Ignatius understood in the context of what it means to be a Christ-follower: Leaders must learn to let go of the need to succeed. We are called to what Frankl describes as a "personal dedication to a cause greater than oneself." For the Christian leader, this is a call to kingdom values. All too often we appeal to "kingdom values" as a cover for our self-absorbed desire. It requires wisdom and courage to bring these false motivations into the light and find the freedom that awaits us!

Inordinate Attachment #3:
The Need for Perfection – Working to Make Things Right

Leaders who are given to perfection as their primary motivation find themselves living in a world that is always in need of correction and reform. Their compulsive energy is continually seeing areas that need attention, and they are always devising ways to improve or transform something or someone. The focus might be on reforming themselves, another person, a program, an organization, a community, or something in the world. They are driven to improve people and things until the "project" reaches a level of perfection, one that will allow their soul to rest. However, that place of rest never comes.

The motivational force of this leader is fixated on getting things *right*. It is said that perfectionists live with an "inner critic"—a relentless voice that is always demanding better. As a result, their heart easily tends to judgmental thoughts because they evaluate everyone based on internal standards of correctness. This inordinate drive to perfectionism can poison the Christian community when it goes unchecked by the leader. It can take shape in many forms. I would suggest three that are most obvious.

First, we know that legalism is a great temptation for the perfectionistic leader who is fixated on people's behavior (moralism). If leaders are not steeped in grace, they will pass along their need to control by setting external standards of conduct and spiritual discipline. The Apostle Paul is regularly seeking to undo this type of perfectionist moralism in his writings. It was insidious in the early church, and it continues to run rampant in contemporary Christian culture. Without realizing it, many Christian leaders are unknowingly motivated by a need to change behavior. Dallas Willard has called this "sin management." Unless the leader is *grace-based* they will give into legalism as their modus operandi.

A second kind of perfectionism that seeks to invade the leader's life and ministry revolves around performance, making excellence the driving goal. This compulsive behavior has numerous targets; the leader might be fixated on the quality of programs, the look of the facility, the production of ministry events, employee performance, and a host of other areas. There is something about the need to control that drives the person in charge to infect everything with a standard of precision and excellence. Leaders who suffer under this type of inordinate affection are compulsively evaluating the situation and the preferred outcomes. The need to fix things takes on an unhealthy level of energy. Obviously, a church or Christian organization is an attractive target for leaders with a driving motivation to fix things. They obsess. Pure motives are lost amid the compulsive need to make things right.

Third, the need for structural reform often sits at the heart of a perfectionistic leader. These people see the world through eyes that call for justice, truthfulness, and integrity. Of course, there are many ministry opportunities that can be designed to address the obvious needs in our broken world (and they are all important). Yet, as good as the work may seem, the motivation may come from the wrong place. Instead of relational union with Christ, and a love for his kingdom, the reforming leader is driven by the need to right the wrongs out of their own need to save others.

In recent years we have witnessed a strong return to a

"missional" emphasis in ministry organizations calling for an increased focus on community involvement and social justice. Such a vision is healthy and God-honoring unless it is precipitated by a perfectionistic leader whose drive to reform is not Spirit-led. We cannot start with the second commandment (love your neighbor) if we have failed to nurture the first commandment (love God). As exciting as the missional movement is, motives must always be evaluated. If they are, we might discover that the energy to engage in a missional focus is faulty.

We have considered three areas where perfectionism might rule the heart of the leader. Repressed anger is the driving force behind this obsession. If it remains unaddressed, the irritation grows as the internal standard and the ideal remains out of reach. When we bring this motivation into the light, we find a deep-rooted inordinate attachment. If the leader is in spiritual direction, the guide is able to lovingly touch the pent-up anger and gently expose the disordered affection through questions and a listening ear.

I know that perfectionism played a role in my need to *over-function* in ministry. A time came when I recognized the treadmill I was on. I have come to love the words of the Canadian folksinger, Leonard Cohen, words that are perfectly suited for perfectionists:

Ring the bells that still can ring
Forget your perfect offering.
There is a crack in everything
That's how the light gets in.[7]

Learning to live with *cracks* in our personal lives, our families, our churches, and our society is a difficult thing for the perfectionist. Cohen calls out: *Forget your perfect offering.* Rather, allow the disappointment to become the place where we rely on the Spirit of God. "There's a crack in everything . . . that's how the light gets in."

The need to be liked.
The need to succeed.
The need to be perfect.

These are just a few of the *inordinate attachments* and *disordered affections* that dominate the landscape of ministry. When leaders function from places of motivation that are twisted, they put themselves at risk. It is impossible to sustain healthy, long-term influence when we start from the wrong place internally.

Sustainable has become a buzzword these days. It is showing up everywhere, including Christian service. If faulty motives are behind a leader's hard work, it is only a matter of time before sustainability breaks down. We have certainly discovered how tempting it is for people to engage in ministry for the wrong reasons, ones that are counterproductive to their spiritual, emotional, and even physical health. (I recently heard of a major health insurer who dropped coverage for a well-known denomination because clergy and their families were such a health risk.[8]) More and more Christian leaders run out of gas before they see the finish line. It's becoming painfully obvious: The way we do ministry is often not sustainable! Faulty motivations must be assessed if we hope to determine what is undermining a healthy soul in the life of the leader.

Our first step toward better practices occurs when we arrive at a core assumption—the need for self-awareness. Once this is in place, healthy patterns of self-care begin to emerge because we can see the places where we sabotage others and ourselves. To find the place of sustainable ministry we will ultimately have to accept the Ignatian strategy to root out inordinate attachments—our twisted motivations. The end goal is true freedom. We are no longer driven by the false self as the primary source of our energy for doing what we do.

Spiritual direction offers us a doorway into the discoveries needed for this type of growth to occur. Over time, the spiritual director discerns those places where the directee is being called to process desires that preempt the primacy of Christ. The director is empowered to gently walk into the soul of the leader and help expose the idolatrous motivations that betray their sense of calling and joy.

If Ignatius were to return to our contemporary ministry scene he would be shocked by the way leaders have given up the "mystery" of knowing Christ for an obsession with effective "management" of his church and other Christian organizations. He would call us back to relational union with Christ. His training program to prepare people for ministry would look radically different than what we find in today's seminary or on the conference circuit. Ignatius knew that effective service flows out of experiential union with Christ. He not only lived this in dramatic fashion, he also helped hundreds of other leaders onto this pathway.

If we're looking for a case study to make spiritual direction applicable in today's world of ministry, Ignatius leads the way. His first agenda would be to help us face the inordinate attachments and disordered affections that hide behind our motivations. These are the secret places that must be processed since they will ultimately sabotage our souls and our call to ministry.

A Spiritual Direction Story
Dave Wilkinson – Church Planter

My first paid ministry job was as a youth pastor in a small rural church. I was nineteen. Four years later, my wife and I moved and I became a youth pastor in a large suburban church. After a long—and mostly successful career—in youth ministry, my wife and I planted a church in downtown Spokane.

I was excited about the challenge and opportunity of doing something different. Our church sent us out with people and money. Over the next year we gathered a team, poured ourselves into the community, watched people come to faith, and launched weekend services. A new church was born.

With all this excitement I became increasingly full of anxiety and depression. Wait, what? New life, new followers of Jesus, new church—and the results were depression and anxiety? I didn't know what was going on, but I knew I needed help. I was with people all the time, but almost never fully present. I was increasingly agitated with my family. Plenty of people would call me a friend, but I was as lonely as I'd ever been. I found it increasingly difficult to pray.

Something needed to change. Every day I fantasized about leaving the ministry. Maybe I could open a pub or get a job at a coffee shop. I was trapped, tired, and lonely.

One weekend I was with some other church planters at a regional training event and the opportunity came up to meet with a spiritual director. I'm not trying to be overly dramatic, but that meeting saved my life. I was able to share my story with somebody who really listened, not just to me but also to the Holy Spirit for me. Through this conversation, and over the next few years, I would begin to know God and myself in a new way. I would begin to recognize when I was relying on my performance as my definition of self. I would begin to see that my motivation for serving, preaching, caring for people, and being a pastor was mostly about me.

What was new about this spiritual direction relationship was the absence of shame as we took a deeper look at my soul. When I am with my director I am able to be poor in spirit. I am able to be a train wreck. I don't have to be competent. I don't have to have answers. I don't have to defend my faith or run from doubt. I get to be me.

What I experience in spiritual direction spills over into other areas. I'm becoming aware of my anxiety before it gets toxic. I'm able to be more present with the people in my life. I'm a better pastor, not because of an arsenal of great tools and techniques, but because of a deep sense that I'm a child of Abba. I still wrestle with anxiety, depression, and loneliness, but I no longer do it alone.

7

Spiritual Discernment:
Understanding Consolation and Desolation

We are ready to move to a second primary theme in Ignatian spirituality, what he called the "discernment of spirits." Ignatius tenaciously addressed this question: "How does someone discern the promptings of God as opposed to the promptings that come from self, or even the devil?" How is it possible for the leader to "keep in step with the Spirit," as we're commanded to do in Galatians 5:25? Ignatius' primary focus became the inner movements of the soul, and through a practice of discernment he helped genuine Christ-followers find the pathway to recognize the voice of God in the middle of all the other desires and distractions roaming in the soul.

Discerning Inner Movements

At the heart of Ignatian spirituality is the conviction that all inner movements in the soul—desires, emotions, promptings, longings, and thoughts—are the experiential place where spiritual discernment is needed. In his own journey, Ignatius found that he regularly encountered interior desires and these inclinations tended to "build up or tear down the Christ-life in us."[1]

He wondered how he should respond to the changing circumstances of life that created the push and pull in his heart. He realized that special insight was needed to differentiate between those movements or voices that were the draw of God and those that were coming from somewhere else—the sinful nature. Paul says it clearly in Romans 7:18–19 when he states: "For I have the desire to do what is good, but I cannot carry it out. For I do not do the good I want to do, but the evil I do not want to do—this I keep on doing." He goes on to talk about two natures or two minds that are at war within him. In other words, we must understand that we are always being pulled in a way that leads us toward God or away from him. The difficult task is to intentionally track these inner movements and learn to process them in ways that lead to health.

For Ignatius, discernment was the "process through which you try to determine whether the development of a thought or commitment proves that it began in God or began somewhere else, and whether the course of action will lead you to God or somewhere else."[2] Jules Toner, in his book, *A Commentary on St. Ignatius's Rules for the Discernment of Spirits*, writes:

> If I am going to hear his [God's] voice, perceive his touch as distinct from all others, open myself to him to do what he wishes, listen and understand so as to respond to whatever he speaks to me, I must cooperate in many ways. I must attend and perceive, listen to and interpret, what he is communicating through my thoughts, impulses, and feelings and through the events to which I am responding.[3]

During his time of convalescence, Ignatius became his own case study in discovering how to discern God's voice from all others. By noting and processing his internal desires and emotions, he developed a strategy whereby he could align himself with God. William Barry states, "Careful attention to inner experience, therefore, is a hallmark of Ignatian spirituality; such attention was absolutely necessary if the individual wants to know God's desires for him or her."[4]

Through careful examination of his own thoughts and feelings, Ignatius developed a series of convictions advising how a sincere follower of Christ could determine the source of inward motivations. This approach, referred to as "the discernment of spirits," has become one of the dominant themes passed down to us through the *Spiritual Exercises*. The *Exercises* demonstrate a primary conviction of Ignatius: "Dedicated persons must become *aware* of the spiritual movements of their hearts, seek to *understand* the origin of these movements . . . and take *action* accordingly."[5]

This method whereby one distinguishes God's voice from all others was built around a series of norms or "rules" which were outlined by Ignatius. These "Rules for the Discernment of Spirits" became the set of instructions that Ignatius developed to help the directee respond to God's leadings. His goal was to teach relational spirituality through the discernment of the Lord's voice. Jesus said that his sheep "listen to his voice" and "know his voice" (John 10:3–4).

Maureen Conroy states, "Although called *rules,* they are really *descriptions* of what happens to people as they relate to God in a personal way. They also serve as *guidelines* for understanding and sifting through experience."[6] Later she adds, "In my growing relationship with God, the Rules have helped me understand more clearly what is happening in my interior life."[7] Making a commitment to process the interior life at those times when our inner being is stirred creates a window for God to guide us and call us closer to himself.

Ignatius believed that if anyone desired, he or she could walk toward union with God, engaging in the same kind of interior work he practiced. He believed that genuine Christ-followers could develop the capacity to process inner feelings and reactions and distinguish the truth from that which is false and misleading. Ignatian spirituality is a profound invitation to take the possibility of existential union with God seriously; it is a call to believe that

God's Spirit resides in our spirit and is continuously relating to us amid all of the experiences life brings. Many leaders fail to pay any attention to the movements in their spirit during the course of the day. They are swept back and forth with no awareness of which "spirit" is prompting the feelings, the impulses, or reactions within. As one leader said to me, "We allow thoughts to run around in our brains rent-free."

With this as a backdrop, a closer look at the Rules is in order, particularly the central theme, which Ignatius refers to as "consolation" and "desolation." Herein we find the key to Ignatius' discernment of spirits.

Consolation and Desolation

In using the terms "consolation" and "desolation," Ignatius focuses on inner movements such as feelings, promptings, longings, and desires. He highlights three facets to help us understand the concept of consolation. It occurs when 1) we find ourselves so aware of the love of God that all other attractions fade in light of a compelling attraction to him, 2) we are deeply saddened and remorseful over sinfulness in our lives and the suffering of Christ on our behalf, and 3) we find something that is strengthening to our faith, hope, and love, leading to interior joy and settledness in God.

Ignatius then highlights what is meant by desolation, which takes place when 1) we feel turmoil in our spirit—a sense of being weighed down, 2) we experience a loss of faith, hope, and love, a resistance to prayer or other spiritual involvement, and 3) we discover movements in our spirit such as despair, rebellion, and selfishness.

Ignatius builds on the premise that movements within the heart of each person tend toward light or darkness, spiritual hope or spiritual disillusionment, emotional well-being or emotional anxiety and fear. He is fully convinced that the spiritual life is one that must be processed in the subjective realm. Maureen Conroy has done excellent work around these themes in her book, *The Discerning Heart*. She offers this:

> The experience of consolation and desolation is the foundation of discernment. Without consolation and desolation there are no inner movements to sift apart; therefore no basis for discernment exists since discernment means to sift through, distinguish, separate and divide interior movements that result from God's personal involvement.[8]

For Ignatius, spiritual direction is centered on the work of helping the directee process the push and pull from within— the many emotions, thoughts, desires, and impulses that roam through the soul throughout the day. Our interior being prompts us in a multitude of directions. Some originate from the work of God's Spirit, and when followed, lead to consolation or a sense of integration. Others come from self or Satan and lead to disintegration, confusion, and compulsion. In the end, they hook us to inordinate attachments or places where freedom is lost. Francis Vanderwall writes:

> The world of the Spirit is as much a part of our daily world as our morning cup of coffee may be. It participates in our world of feelings, inner inclinations, hopes, visions and dreams. It is the very stuff that our daily routines are made of, for in the Spirit's cajolings, urgings, and scoldings many a daily action receives its motivation. The world of the spirits is comprised of both good and bad movements. We learn to distinguish them and differentiate the one from the other by looking for the symptoms within us.[9]

The work of discerning various movements and the symptoms within us will, once again, nurture experiential union with God. He makes himself known if we will take time to discern his voice from that of the enemy.

Jules Toner has written one of the most comprehensive works on this aspect of Ignatian spirituality. He sums up consolation in this way: "Spiritual consolation means for Ignatius an experience in which living faith is not only increased but is recognized by the believer . . . it issues in feelings of peace, joy, contentment, confidence, exultation and the like."[10] His description of desolation is equally as helpful. Desolation becomes evident in the:

> . . . thoughts and affective acts and feelings which are contrary to those which living faith of itself tend to generate. These motions . . . tend in some measure toward loss of confidence in God's love and care for us. Thus, by degrees of discouragement, they tend toward making one despair of ever achieving the goal that had sprung from living faith. When these anti-spiritual movements so dominate some area of conscious life that the feelings of peace and joy flowing from living faith are suppressed, or are drowned out by feelings of anxiety, sadness and discouragement *regarding faith life*, then the person experiences spiritual desolation.[11]

Thus, Ignatius contended that, in our subjective experience, we are regularly encountering feelings, movements, or impulses that nurture spiritual optimism (joy, hope, peace, freedom, centeredness, balance, and courage) and others that breed spiritual pessimism (apathy, guilt, compulsion, disorder, rigidity, perfectionism, and resistance).

It might be helpful to highlight an inner movement that I have experienced and struggled with all of my life. Sometimes I feel like I am permanently stuck like a needle in the scratch of an old vinyl record album. It is certainly desolation and, unless I name it, this thought runs around "rent-free." So here it is: I often experience a deep sense of inadequacy (let's be honest . . . shame) as if I am not good enough for God. Behind that feeling is the belief that God doesn't like me. I know he loves me—but like me? That's different. My deepest longing is to know God likes me, that he takes pleasure in me as one friend to another. This is the kind of relationship we all truly desire, not some platonic union where we are told we are loved but never celebrate the sheer joy of knowing that love experientially. My feelings of inadequacy rob me of all the joy intended in my union with God. It's pretty obvious that this would be the voice of desolation (not God speaking)—right? Yet why do I regularly assume (and feel) this is God's voice and that he is expressing disappointment toward me like an unhappy parent?

If Ignatius were to speak into the spiritual issues surrounding this inner push in my soul, he would seek to help me recognize the voice of desolation and reject it. However, rejecting it is easier said than done. When desolation embeds itself as the "voice of God," it takes considerable work to name it, process it, and reject it.

I must pay close attention to my inner movements (feelings) and the resulting thoughts that are generated in my mind. False guilt and shame can often be mistaken as conviction and therefore wrongly interpreted as the voice of God. The false nature of this inner movement is exposed when we understand that it drives us into ourselves with shame rather than out of ourselves and into God's grace. An effective spiritual director will ask questions of the directee to help the person distinguish these movements (toward or away from God) and help them to use these movements to establish deeper union with Christ.

Even though the discernment of spirits seems to be an obvious pathway for any believer to attend to—and particularly a leader—most people fail to process these inner leanings. In

Protestant evangelicalism, most spiritual formation stays focused in the realm of thoughts, information, and then behavior. Little or no consideration is given to the subjective realm. Philip Sheldrake contends, "In western countries we have fostered the intellect and despised the emotions, thus becoming more cerebral than sensitive." He goes on to say that the "experience of consolation-desolation is not easy for us today, because the pace of life and our very conceptual education can so easily keep us out of touch with ourselves."[12]

When we study the scripture, we find that the Hebrew people connected their emotions to their spirituality in day-to-day experience. When talking of the condition of the soul, they regularly used emotional descriptors to process their spiritual journey. According to the Old Testament saints, the soul can be anguished, grieved, distressed, bitter, and weary, as well as restored, joyful, delighted, satisfied, and resting. There are many cultures that, similar to the Jewish people, seem to live closer to their emotions. However, Christians in the Western world demonstrate a loss of the importance of this vital component in the spiritual journey.

When we minimize or deny our feelings, we are actually distorting what it means to bear the personal image of God. Dan Allender and Tremper Longman pick up on the Ignatian theme regarding the importance of our emotions and write, "We are to listen to and ponder what we feel in order to be moved to the far deeper issue of what our hearts are doing with God and others."[13] Feelings and moods, as well as impressions and even fantasies, are not irrelevant. If we hope to forge new territory in calling leaders into a deeper union with Christ, one that is personal and experiential, it is critical that we learn to process emotion as a primary place where God's Spirit is interfacing with ours. Kathleen Fischer says, "Bringing hidden and unacknowledged emotion to awareness frequently leads to breakthroughs on the spiritual journey."[14]

I often conduct retreats with leaders. One of the exercises

I present is a careful review of an extended list of emotions. At a recent retreat with about twenty leaders, we completed this exercise by putting a checkmark beside all the dominant emotions each person had experienced in the past month or two. I passed out a list of over 200 words that describe emotions. (Yes! There are more than 200! If you want an extended list, just Google "list of emotions." You'll have all you need.) I then asked them to choose an emotion that was dominating their life experience and write it down. Here are the ones they highlighted:

Overwhelmed	Grateful	Impatient
Burdened	Determined	Confused
Discouraged	Distracted	Grieving
Misunderstood	Optimistic	Wounded
Anxious	Drained	Lonely
Overwhelmed	Empty	Overwhelmed

If you look at this list carefully, you might ask, "Did you pass out an inventory of negative emotions, because the responses are dominated by a lot of difficult feelings?" No, there was a long list of happy emotions to choose from: excited, energized, loved, gratified, joyful, appreciated, confident, and more than thirty others. Furthermore, while the list included two hundred emotional descriptors, three people chose the word "overwhelmed". You might assume that these leaders were weary from a lifetime of ministry. Actually, they were all young pastors, mostly in their twenties and thirties.

If you were a soul friend to one of these leaders, in what direction would you take the conversation as they processed a difficult emotion? Would you simply give advice? Or would you listen to their soul and explore these emotions as interior movements carefully seeking to help the individual determine what's behind the emotion—consolation or desolation? Are the impulses generated by the voice of *God*? Might this be the voice of *self*? Or could it be the voice of the enemy playing into the situation?

Discernment and Spiritual Direction

Understanding the importance of discernment—learning to differentiate the leadings that come from God versus those that lead away from him—is fundamental to the practice of guiding others. Central to spiritual direction is the process of "discerning the spiritualizing influence of God with the directee as manifested in and through his/her thoughts, feelings, desires, aspirations, activities and relationships."[15]

In my own practice of spiritual direction with leaders, I have sought to follow the insights offered by Ignatius in this area. A leader will often arrive for spiritual direction fixated on a ministry problem or issue related to his or her leadership. Emotion spills out, and behind that is a desire for advice—a way to resolve the leadership problem. However, as we go further into the session, I shift gears and ask where the individual senses that God might be at work in the haze and tangle of his or her ministry. What are the emotions revealing about their spiritual journey? How is God seeking to form them?

I resonate with what Gerald Grosh writes:

Gradually the person recognizes those impulses which lead to greater negativity and those which lead to greater freedom. As he begins to distinguish these impulses, the director helps him associate God with the latter movement and a non-God force with the former. The director helps the person focus upon the Lord and not on himself, experientially looking beyond those things which he dislikes. Here the director's role shifts from teacher to guide. He leads the person to a knowledge and experience of the true God.[16]

Ignatius understood one other critical aspect of the role of emotion in the process of spiritual direction. In the *Exercises* he sought to mobilize emotion for good by inviting the directee to pray for sorrow, tears, affliction, amazement, love, gladness, and tranquility. Ignatius did not underestimate a person's emotional matrix as a central aspect of spiritual formation. In one sense, he was hundreds of years ahead of his time in that he understood the role and power of emotion in the individual's life. He harnessed the subjective side of life to forge a dynamic and personal model of spirituality.

As a director works with a leader, the deepest spiritual longings of his or her heart will surface. When revealed, there will be a sense of emotion, usually an ache or a longing, that needs to be called forth. The director is called to walk with the directee into these deep spiritual longings and, in the words of Ignatius, "Ask God for what I want and desire." In so doing, the directee will be using his or her emotions as a pathway to pursue God.

We are now living in a time when the subjective or experiential side of life has surfaced with such intensity that it has become the primary force shaping the spiritual horizon of our culture. People are searching for God, but they have lost interest in theological information and religious institutionalism as the framework for their pursuit. Believing that there is something more, they crave firsthand knowledge; the actual experience of God matters most.

The Ignatian emphasis on the subjective and interior life as the place where one can know Christ, coupled with his strong commitment to the authority of scripture and the sovereignty of Christ over all things, should lead us to give serious consideration to the *Spiritual Exercises* as a pathway to authentic spirituality. Ignatius offers us a place to rediscover spiritual passion and engage in experiential discovery while also providing a biblically sound and disciplined structure. The *Spiritual Exercises*, although they are almost five hundred years old, invite contemporary followers of

Christ to move past those barriers that prevent them from realizing their spiritual hopes—hopes they have had for so long, but were never realized.

In my own experience I have been particularly struck with the importance of tracking my inner movements and seeking to discern those that foster union with God and those that draw me away from him. In so doing, I have been surprised by numerous movements that otherwise would go unnoticed. Additionally, I have discovered how I am often pulled in a way that would seem to come from God, until I realize the un-freedom that surrounds this voice. By practicing discernment, I am able to stop certain assumptions in my thoughts that usually lead toward spiritual frustration and guilt—desolation.

Much has been written about the discernment of spirits, specifically the importance of consolation and desolation, yet most of this literature remains unread in the Protestant evangelical tradition. Recovering the principles that Ignatius learned through his experience leads the believer toward a spiritual union, one that most people long for but no longer expect to find.

A Spiritual Direction Story
Rita Nussli – Associate Director, SoulFormation (Former Executive Director, New Horizons Ministries)

While I grew up in a strong Christian home as a pastor's daughter, it was at age twenty-one that I began to deeply embrace my relationship with God. I obtained a Master's degree in Social Work and at the age of thirty I became the executive director of New Horizons Ministries, serving homeless and street-involved youth in Seattle.

During the first three years as executive director I led this ministry with minimal attention to the needs of my own soul. Fifteen minutes with Oswald Chambers in *My Utmost for His Highest* was my only source of guidance and strength. I gave birth to my son at age thirty-three and began the complicated journey of balancing motherhood, family life, and ministry obligations. Within six months I was exhausted. I had little confidence that Jesus' words were possible: "Come to me, all you who are weary and burdened, and I will give you rest . . . my yoke is easy and my burden is light" (Matthew 11:28–30). As I neared the crisis point, I set aside a day to "hear" from God about my exhaustion in his service.

On that day Oswald Chambers' focus was on Matthew 11:28–30. He emphasized that many of us concentrate on God's promise that the yoke would be easy while ignoring the invitation to "come" to him. A light bulb went off in my head and heart as I realized my need to "come." This meant spending more time alone with God, and my reading shifted toward books written by the early saints who practiced the spiritual disciplines. What followed was a journey to find a spiritual director, someone who would help me apply what I was learning.

Before I found a spiritual director, I found two other women leaders who I met with monthly and we became a spiritual direction group of three. We prayed, listened carefully for God's direction, and spoke Holy Spirit-guided truth into each other's ministry and personal lives. Coming together with a focus on mutual direction helped us grow in powerful ways both spiritually and as leaders.

When I chose a spiritual director she walked beside me in many areas of transformation. A critical issue was where my sense of worth came from. I found it challenging to set needed limits for the staff and ministry because of my worry about being rejected or disliked.

As my spiritual director and I listened together to God, I began to trust and lead out of the knowledge that I am God's beloved daughter. With increased certainty that my value did not come from ministry success or the approval of staff, I became able to make tough leadership decisions. The ability to self-differentiate who I was created to be from my role as executive director was firmly established through this work done in partnership with my spiritual director.

My director would sit with me each month and listen to my struggles in leadership and life. Gently, she would ask questions that brought me back to a place of hearing God's voice. We pursued listening to his voice as I grew in my longing to become transformed into the image of Jesus. The journey into spiritual direction reoriented the direction of my ministry. Listening came before doing. Spiritual direction nurtured intimacy with Christ out of which service would flow.

During the next eighteen years, my experience in learning to listen with my spiritual director impacted the way I led. I partnered with a prayer team for me personally and for the street ministry. The executive leadership team, along with the staff and the board, learned to listen to God and discern his direction. We were intent on discovering God's will before jumping into a strategic plan. Personal retreat days created space for staff to pursue intimacy with God and guidance for service. "Being" preceded "doing."

I spent twenty-two years as the executive director of New Horizons. What started as a desperate search to survive in ministry led me to the spiritual disciplines and a spiritual director who would help me understand how to practice them in ways that were fitting to my temperament and pattern of life. These discoveries spilled over onto our team, leading us to a place of deep intimacy with God and spiritual discernment in our ministry plan.

8

Strengthening the Foundation: Critical Themes

A careful study of Ignatius leads to the discovery of numerous other critical themes that guide the leader to freedom and spiritual formation. So far we have looked at his focus on "motives" (inordinate attachments) and "discernment" (consolation and desolation). These themes represent places of entry when conducting spiritual direction, like windows that open during conversation if we are truly listening to one another. These reoccurring focal points in the *Exercises* have become firmly established as proven pathways to spiritual health and freedom.

What follows in this chapter are six additional themes developed by Ignatius that were derived through his personal experience and his journey toward offering spiritual direction to the many other leaders who sought guidance. These topics present valuable potential for understanding spiritual formation and direction with Christian leaders. For those who are called to provide the ministry of soul friendship, the following concepts represent the pathway toward conversations that form the leader's soul.

Experiential Union with Christ

The driving heartbeat, which remains central to everything

Ignatius desired to foster, is experiential union with Christ. For too long the church has had a strategy and practice of spiritual formation that leans heavily toward the cognitive side of spiritual formation. Ignatius maintained that the primary focus of spiritual direction is *experiential* union in a person's relationship with God.

This cognitive or informational approach as the paradigm under which we seek to shape the believer's journey has run dry and become one of the key reasons why so many pastors are struggling. We live in a day when the desire for spiritual experience is emphasized in almost every corner of church life. People are looking for more. The relevance of Ignatian spirituality in today's world is unusually pertinent because it offers such a theologically sound foundation for experiential union with God.

It's not uncommon to hear Christian leaders ask the question, "Would you like to have a personal relationship with God?" However, one wonders whether, in most cases, Christian leaders would have to admit that "personal" is simply not an accurate word to describe their own encounters with God. All too often we hold out the possibility of something amazingly wonderful even though we have little or no knowledge of this in our spiritual lives. For Ignatius, this personal relationship was his deepest quest.

Since God is a self-revealing God, we can look for his hand in all of life's experiences. His Spirit lives in our spirit as the guide, or the interpreter, of God's intentions. Through discernment, we can join the Spirit and come to the realization that God is making himself known. As we have learned, Ignatius believed that God's Spirit is always moving within the heart of the individual, and awareness of these movements opens the door to a moment-by-moment encounter with God.

As we turn to the scriptures, we find an obvious confirmation of this experiential emphasis. The work of God in the Bible is personal, individual, internal, and emotional. Moses, David, Isaiah,

John, and Paul are dynamically engaged in their walk with God. They move beyond cognitive knowledge and into a union that is transformational. It is certainly evident that today's churches are filled with people who long for this type of union with God. Gary Moon, psychologist and spiritual director, writes:

> The point is this; it seems that many in the Christian world have recently reawakened to the truth that wearing the label, "Christian," is not synonymous with experiencing the intimate, moment by moment relationship with God that souls were designed to enjoy, and have begun to place hope in the practice of spiritual direction as a methodology for finding the way to a more abundant life. Across denominational barriers, there seems to be a tidal wave of interest in learning how to experience intimate friendship with God.[1]

Throughout the history of the church we are admonished by great spiritual masters to avoid settling for less than firsthand knowledge of God. A. W. Tozer, someone whose writings appeal to personal encounter, joins Ignatius by stating: "We have almost forgotten that God is a person and, as such, can be cultivated as any person can."[2] In his book, *The Pursuit of God*, Tozer invites the seeker toward existential union with God: "In making himself known to us he [God] stays by the familiar pattern of personality. . . . The continuous and unembarrassed interchange of love and thought between God and the soul of the redeemed man is the throbbing heart of New Testament religion."[3] Individuals who enter spiritual direction are choosing to process the potential for— and the reality of—experiential union with God.

This aspect of Ignatian spirituality is critical if Christian leaders hope to sustain passion in ministry. As overseers we find ourselves involved in all kinds of sacred and holy activities while, at the same time, we ourselves may lack a sense of intimacy with God. This contradiction will wreck the soul. If we hope to avoid disillusionment and burnout in ministry, it is critical that we find places where our experience—or lack thereof—is placed on the table and we are able to talk about it freely. The time has come for Christian leaders to model what it means to process spiritual experience in relationship. Spiritual direction is the door to these conversations. Barry and Connolly believe that "experience is to spiritual direction what foodstuff is to cooking. Without foodstuff there can be no cooking. Without religious experience there can be no spiritual direction."[4]

Finding God in All Things

The desire for experiential union takes us to another theme that Ignatius believed was central to growth in our spiritual experience. A phrase frequently associated with Ignatius' life and writings is "finding God in all things."[5] As we have already learned, Ignatius was a "contemplative in action," so he taught that union with God could be fostered at any time and under any circumstances. In his spiritual diary, written near the end of his life, Ignatius states the following: "Every time, any hour, that he wished to find God, he found him."[6] After almost five hundred years, this truth continues to resound in devotional literature. Elisabeth-Paule Labat writes, "God is in fact always pressing into the everyday and often colorless fabric of the life of each one of us."[7]

We live in a culture of busyness, particularly religious busyness for pastors and Christian leaders. Often, such leaders capitulate to a life of distraction, resulting in a complete loss of spiritual focus amid the many responsibilities of serving others. While Ignatius encouraged periods of solitude, he was more deeply concerned with how one maintains a sense of God's presence during the challenges of the day. In this sense, he was a "mystic of action in tune with the one action of God."[8] Central to Ignatius' practice was the belief that "unless we are contemplative we will miss God acting in everything around us and in ourselves."[9]

So often we divorce contemplation from action. We divorce them so completely that we make no attempt to establish union with God throughout the day. We slip into the belief that the time for spiritual encounter comes when we stop for what is usually called "devotions" or "quiet time." It is important for us to realize that contemplation and action are not disconnected from each other, and the life of Christ is full of examples in which we see them joined together.

Throughout history others have emphasized the possibility of finding God in the middle of life's circumstances. Brother Lawrence offered us his experience as a model for such intentionality in his book, *The Practice of the Presence of God.* He wrote, "The most holy and necessary practice in our life is the presence of God."[10] Jean-Pierre de Caussade emphasized the "sacrament of the present moment."[11] His thesis was simply this: "The events of every moment are stamped with the will of God."[12] Thomas Kelly, in his book, *A Testament to Devotion,* wrote about the Inner Principle—a continual awareness of God in the soul. "Deep within us all there is an amazing inner sanctuary of the soul. . . . Eternity is in our hearts, pressing upon our time-worn lives, warming us with intimations of an astounding destiny, calling us home to Itself."[13] This principle of "awareness" is a necessary point of discussion when we turn to an understanding of spiritual direction.

Gary Moon and David Benner share a story about a group of leaders who were just beginning to discover this Ignatian concept. They write:

> These were long-term, card-carrying members of evangelicalism who had spent their lifetimes in Christian study and service. But only recently, it seemed, had each enrolled in Christianity 101. . . . Toward the end of our time together, one of the group members uttered words that seem an appropriate summary to that discussion:

"Could it be that it [the process of spiritual formation] is simply becoming aware that God is everywhere and then learning how to be with him—in the presence of divine love?"[14]

Such awareness is critical to the well-being of the leader, and spiritual direction becomes the logical place to process all of life in light of God's presence. Barry and Connolly encourage this as a central aspect of working with others:

What are the most fundamental tasks of the director? Let us propose there are two, and that they issue from this insight: the contemplative core of all prayer and of all Christian life is conscious relationship with God. The tasks are: First, helping the directee pay attention to God as he reveals himself; second, helping the directee recognize his reactions and decide on his response to God.[15]

The director is continually seeking to address the issue of Christ's presence in the life of the directee. Where is God making himself known, and how can we recognize his hand in our life? Jean Laplace reinforces the same starting place in spiritual direction. He writes:

What we should wish is for discernment to be applied not only to those moments of privileged solitude when we meet God in the prayer of the desert, but to everything that makes up the daily warp and woof of our existences. Events, as we say today, are the signs of God. Direction should train us to recognize them.[16]

At the heart of spiritual direction is an essential question, which is asked by the director: "Where have you sensed the presence of Christ in your life?" The goal is to help the directee reflect and discern how Christ has been evident. Often this type of work is counterintuitive. We find Christ in unexpected places.[17]

Such was the Ignatian journey toward God—one of reflective evaluation. The Ignatian commitment to awareness is central to an experiential union with Christ. Unless we take time to honor his presence in all that surrounds us, we will miss his attempts to establish union with us.

It is important to add one more thought at this point. Often, when I begin spiritual direction with a Christian leader, the primary issue the directee brings is one related to ministry challenges or church leadership. It might be a staffing concern, a relational conflict, a financial problem, a major decision, or something that relates to management. I am struck by how organizational concerns dominate the landscape of a leader's life. It is as if they are looking at our time together as a place for coaching rather than spiritual direction.

While it is important to start where the directee wants to start, I have discovered that the spiritual director must be committed to the importance of what I call "going beneath the water line." By this I mean that sooner or later amid all the talk over the organizational issues, the director must ask, "What do you think all of this is saying about your journey with Christ?" Something very important happens at this point. The conversation now shifts from doing to being, from the problem in the organization to the leader's relationship with Christ.

Ignatius' principle of "finding God in all things" relates directly to each and every thing that happens in life—marriage, family, finances, career, desires, health, emotions, suffering, success, failure, as well as our life in ministry. However, unless the spiritual director goes beneath the water line, we may find ourselves functioning as coaches or self-help therapists who fail to connect the dots between the experiences of everyday life and the work of God in the soul of the directee.

The Value and Use of Imagination

Ignatius believed that a primary pathway into the biblical texts and experiential encounter with Christ was through the use of imagination. He discovered the value of this when he lay wounded in Loyola. While previously he had imagined exploits in service of an earthly king or queen, he now found himself using these powers in the discovery and service of Christ. This active use of his imagination became fully developed as a tool to encounter Jesus.

Ignatius taught the use of this approach by training spiritual directors to assign certain gospel stories and texts to the directee, ones that seemed suited to their spiritual life and needs at the time. During the daily reflections while on a retreat, the individual spent extended time moving into the story with the intention of having face-to-face encounters with Christ. The participants were encouraged to enter into the biblical text experientially—to touch, taste, smell, see, and hear the event as if they were actually there. The goal was to encounter Christ in the salvation story rather than just to know it.

The centrality of this imaginative component leads to a definition of Ignatian spirituality as "kataphatic" in nature. While other mystics believed God was encountered through the letting-go of conscious thought (referred to as "apophatic"), the kataphatic approach invites us into the active use of our mind.[18] The directee is invited to listen to conversations, notice facial responses, and enter into the feelings of each person, especially Christ.

> The imaginative representation is a way, much like a movie, to help us compose our whole being and to open ourselves to the action of the Holy Spirit mediated by the Word. This is necessary, because Jesus entered the world of space and time; and we ourselves exist multi-dimensionally as body-persons.[19]

While the imagination is often seen as a dangerous place of departure from sound doctrine and practice, in Ignatian spirituality it is actually a place where scripture and Christology shine. According to John Dister, "The *Exercises* assume that the pattern of Christ's life is the pattern for the growth and development of the spiritual life of the Christian."[20]

This is the genius of the *Exercises*, an amazing balance between experiential encounter and the objective use of the scriptures as the basis for any such an encounter. It was through the imagination that the individual could release all constraints and enter the biblical story. In doing so they discover Christ in a way that brings healing to the distorted views held in their understanding. We encounter Jesus as someone who treats us like a friend and brother.

Ignatius taught that transformational change occurred at a feeling level and involves much more than a cognitive response. His goal was the use of imaginative power around the objective truth of God's Word to lead the individual into a direct encounter with Christ. Regarding the use of imagination, Tad Dunne writes, "Although most people today find it strange at first to enter into historical scenes through their imagination, the majority of those who try it find the practice surprisingly full of real assets."[21]

In my own journey I have pursued the practice of imagination around particular gospel stories and have found this to be a profound experience. Entering into the story truly does lead to processing with Christ in personal ways, opening windows of transformation. Recently I was imagining the story of the four men who lowered the paralyzed man through the roof. I was standing beside Jesus when he said, "Your sins are forgiven." The power of hearing those words penetrated my soul. I let Jesus say the same words to me— *your sins are forgiven.* What a sweet gift!

Somehow, somewhere along the way the church became suspicious of imagination as a valuable pathway to encountering Christ.

It was as if imagination was off-limits—it fell into the category of "new age practices" that might lead a person away from objective truth. However, if believers could rediscover the value of imagining the historical texts of Christ's life, they would simply be living into the scriptures at an experiential level. Ignatius encouraged this. It was his firm belief that truth needed to touch the emotions.

Recovering the use of imagination is difficult for adults who have learned to live in a rational world where anything imaginative is categorized as unproductive—even childish. In our results-driven culture we have lost the art of imagining ourselves in the story. It will take effort to recover our childlike capacity for imagination. The starting place is simply to follow Ignatius' directives: Choose a narrative from the life of Christ and dwell in it until you are watching, touching, eating, and breathing in all that goes on. Become part of the story. Discover the power of being there!

Self-Awareness and the Discipline of *Examen*

The *Spiritual Exercises* are designed to help the individual develop the skills needed to "wake up" to the motives and inner realities that deceive the heart in ways that bind and blind. Ignatius believed the pathway to heightened awareness of self before God was through what he called *examen*. He emphasized *examen* as the one prayer that must be engaged in every day; it is central to finding God in all things. William Barry describes this practice as follows:

> We meet God at every moment of the day, but we are not always aware of his reality. Thus, each period of the day can be considered a "period of prayer," a time when we meet God. The examen, then, becomes a period of reflection on a particular period of a day in order to become aware of the touch of God.[22]

Rose Mary Dougherty writes, "[We] look back with God at the

events and relationships of each day. . . . We ask God's perspective on what has been going on. It's like sitting down with God and watching a video of our day, with God as the commentator."[23] Through *examen* we pray for the grace of a deep knowledge of our sins. Ignatius believed that watchfulness is the real guide of the soul. Additionally, George Aschenbrenner reminds us that, "This radical reorientation is not easy for anyone. In practice, a man or woman is asked to be in every way suspicious and distrustful of every aspect of the motivation behind their actions, to be willing to explore and reorient this motivation."[24]

Learning how to maintain a reflective state of mind as you move through the events of your life is certainly a spiritual discipline that takes time to learn. *Examen* is practicing this reflective pattern; it is the Ignatian way of looking back and holding ourselves, and the pattern of our lives, in the presence of God. Tad Dunne refers to this as "the practice of noticing."[25] It means stopping long enough, in the words of John Baillie, to "ponder the pattern my life is weaving."[26]

This principle of self-awareness and the practice of *examen* are critical to the health of the Christian leader. All too often, individuals are living with little or no awareness of the false self or the shadow side of their lives. In addition, there is a tendency to move through our days without any sense of gratitude, without noticing the beauty and love that fill each experience. Instead, leaders remain submerged in their professional roles. The sin of twisted motives may hide behind much of their work and lead to compulsive patterns and behavior. Breaking free necessitates that interior work is practiced. When a leader makes *examen* a regular part of life, he or she is shocked to see the unaddressed issues that have been lying beneath the surface. Ignatius was certain that if we came with a humble heart, the end result would be a poverty of spirit that sets the stage for the deepest sense of God's forgiveness and love.

Examen is built on the principle of self-awareness, something that spiritual directors are cognizant of in the process of working with the individual. This represents another unusual strength of Ignatian spirituality: It is grounded in a thoroughly biblical framework coupled with an understanding of the psychological nature of humanity. Throughout the history of the church, this concept of "double knowledge" (knowledge of God and self) has been emphasized by noted leaders as an essential component for spiritual formation.

In his classic work, *Confessions*, Augustine prayed, "Grant, Lord, that I may know myself that I may know thee."[27] Meister Eckhart, the Dominican mystic of the thirteenth century wrote, "No one can know God who does not first know himself."[28] And, at the same time Ignatius was exploring this "double knowledge," John Calvin (1530) wrote this in the opening words of his *Institutes of the Christian Religion*: "There is no deep knowing of God without a deep knowing of self, and no deep knowing of self without a deep knowing of God."[29] While other great spiritual guides taught this truth, it was Ignatius who modeled it in his personal experience and then communicated it to others in the *Exercises*.

In conclusion, to practice *examen* we may need some help in understanding the process. The *examen* traditionally involves the following five steps (offered by the Parish of St. Ignatius of Loyola).[30]

1. *Recall you are in the presence of God.* No matter where you are, you are a creature in the midst of creation and the Creator who called you forth is concerned for you.

2. *Give thanks to God for favors received.* Pause and spend a moment looking at this day's gifts. Take stock of what you received and gave. Notice these clues that guide living.

3. *Ask for awareness of the Holy Spirit's aid.* Before you explore the mystery of the human heart, ask to receive the Holy Spirit so you can look upon your actions and motives with honesty and patience. The Spirit gives a freedom to look upon yourself without condemnation or complacency and thus be open to growth.

4. *Now examine how you are living this day.* Recalling the events of your day, explore the context of your actions. Review the day, hour-by-hour, searching for the internal events of your life. Ask what you were involved in and who you were with, and review your hopes and hesitations. What moved you to act the way you did?

5. *Pray words of reconciliation and resolve.* Having reviewed this day of your life, look upon yourself with compassion and see your need for God. Realize God's manifestations of concern for you. Express sorrow for sin, give thanks for grace, and praise God for the times you responded in ways that allowed you to better see God in your life.

Understanding and Processing Our Desires

Ignatius believed that desires played a critical role in helping the individual toward an experiential relationship with Christ. Through his own personal journey, and then in the *Exercises*, he developed what has been called a "paradigm of the spirituality of desire."[31] At the beginning of each of the *Exercises*, Ignatius invites the retreatant to "ask for what I want." Over and over again, he encourages us to look for those deepest longings and tune them toward God. Janet Ruffing says, "What do we really want? Human and divine desiring is a core feature of the spiritual life. Our desires energize the spiritual quest and lead us to God."[32]

Kevin Moore, trained in the field of psychology and counseling writes, "Specific desires and wants should be identified according to St. Ignatius. . . . [O]nce named, these true desires become allied with the revealed desire of God for us."[33] When Ignatius invites us to ask for the one thing we desire, he is actually calling us to take a closer look at our deepest longings and discover that they are ultimately linked to God himself. When the *Exercises* prompt us to formulate our desire into a spiritual passion, we discover that we are to ask for what we truly desire in order to be in touch with our true longings for God, longings which run at the center of our being.[34]

William Reiser, quoting Julian of Norwich, referred to this core desire as "the wound of sincere longing."[35] He goes on to say, "If you can help someone get in touch with this core desire—the native restlessness of the heart—then you have helped that person on their way to God."[36]

Long before contemporary psychology was on the scene, Ignatius was wrestling with the passions, feelings, and longings that shape a person's life. His goal was to understand these forces and discover how they played into one's spiritual journey. When one begins to understand the Ignatian emphasis on desires, one can see that he was not interested in behavioral change; Ignatius was set upon relational change. He believed transformation occurs at a heart level, when one begins to truly understand how his or her deepest longings are directly connected to God himself.

A constant refrain running through the whole of the *Exercises* is the invitation to pray for what you desire. The whole experience happens on the level of desire of the heart. Ignatius believes that desire, as the deepest, most personal experience of grace, always reveals a person's true identity and is the birthplace of commitment.[37]

In this sense, we see that all desire, even that which has been twisted, can be processed and, ultimately, understood to be something that has potential to be directed toward spiritual health. In the end, all desires lead us toward God. Stinissen believes we are on the wrong path regarding our desire when desire has gone its own way—"when it forms a tributary instead of letting its waters stream in the deep, broad riverbed that leads to the sea."[38] A key purpose of spiritual direction is to help the individual recognize desire and assist him or her to integrate those desires into the need for God. The goal is to listen to a person's longing and then to help him or her explore it—to identify and solidify it with a view to developing his or her relationship with God.[39]

With this in mind, it would be difficult to engage in spiritual direction with someone who shows no desire, who has no longing. Ignatius believed that deep and intense passion is what drives the heart toward God. Our deepest and truest desires are God-given. Janet Ruffing writes:

> Many Christians never entertain their desires long enough to know what they really want. If we habitually suppress our wants, we may never discover the true core of our longing that could lead us more deeply into God. It takes courage to allow our desires to become conscious.[40]

This neglect of our desires is something not uncommon within the evangelical tradition of spirituality. All too often we have frowned upon desire, placing it in the "dangerous" category along with other subjective experiences. John Eldredge states, "Many committed Christians are wary about getting in touch with their desires . . . because they fear that they will discover some dark hunger lurking in their heart."[41]

A starting place in spiritual direction is to help the directee realize what he or she really wants. Many leaders have lost desire for one reason or another. Some have held unfulfilled desire in their relationship with God for so long that they now suppress it. Facing spiritual disappointments by allowing long-lost idealism to surface is simply too painful for some leaders. Yet, deep underneath, they would like to dream again. Spiritual direction is a wonderful pathway to recover true desire and God-given motivation upon which sustainable ministry is fostered.

Holy Indifference and Decision-Making

My wife and I spent three hours with a younger couple who were facing a significant decision. They were being asked to apply for an international ministry position. The issue on the table was stated: "Was now the time to follow the sense of calling we've had for years—to serve cross-culturally?" Leaving would have been incredibly difficult. They had a young son with a daughter soon to be born. Family members lived close by and loved them dearly. They were currently serving in pastoral roles and had established significant influence as leaders.

At one point in the evening I suggested the value of the Ignatian principle referred to as "holy indifference." Ignatius believed this is the pathway to freedom and to the true discovery of being centered in God's will. Holy indifference means we come to a place where our interior attitude is one of complete openness. We are willing to do whatever God wills. There are no boxes marked "private;" instead we have released any agendas or inclinations to manipulate the outcome to suit our hopes. In our interior being the first priority is to know we are where God wants us to be.[42] Karl Rahner contends: "This distance from things is a goal that must always be re-won again and again."[43]

As soon as I mentioned "holy indifference" I could see a connection on the face of the woman who sat across the table. It was as if everything became easier. The burden of having to make a decision—the right decision—was lifted. What mattered was attitude, not outcome.

Before a leader was welcomed into the Jesuit Order, Ignatius required the individual to participate in a thirty-day retreat to discern if this decision was truly God's will for his life. He knew the individual was making a life-altering choice. Together they walked through the *Spiritual Exercises* one step at a time. The starting point was moving to the place of "holy indifference." At the beginning of the *Spiritual Exercises*, he wrote:

> For it is necessary to make ourselves indifferent to all created things in all that is allowed to the choice of our free will and is not prohibited to it; so that, on our part, we want not health rather than sickness, riches rather than poverty, honor rather than dishonor, long rather than short life, and so, in all the rest; desiring and choosing only what is most conducive for us to the end for which we are created.[44]

Ignatius established a fundamental principle that would set the stage for making decisions in line with God's will. The concept of holy indifference involves "naming and laying aside anything that will deter the person or group from focusing on God's will as the ultimate value."[45] When we reach this state of interior freedom, we care about the outcome in a way that leaves everything wide open for God to act. There is a confidence that settles in because we have a deep sense his sovereignty is being honored in a way that ensures the best outcome.

Holy indifference is always a journey. It is central to our spiritual formation when we find ourselves in the decision-making process. As we move through the season of discernment we will bump up against hopes and assumptions that must be released in order to move back to the place of freedom. Often, we will find ourselves saying, "Yes, but . . ." as we try to fully release that which holds us hostage. This process of decision-making is often

God's way of exposing the assumptions we hold—ones that are not in line with his purposes. We discover that, even though we sincerely want God's will, we have exceptions that remain hidden in our soul. Ignatius believed that following God meant rigorously tracking down those assumptions and returning to the place of freedom. The only way to get there is to set your sights on holy indifference and the choice to release any and all objections.

I often meet people who carry significant stress related to a particular decision. It seems perfectly acceptable, yet it's not. Something is overriding their ability to come to a place of internal peace, even before the decision is made. Usually that "something" is the deep desire to maintain control, thus ensuring the best outcome. Often, a type of perfectionism rules as the individual continues to fear they might not make the right choice.

Once a sincere follower is able to understand and experience the freedom that comes with holy indifference, they are capable of sensing when their inner being is off balance. Life is filled with decisions. To learn the joy and peace of "releasing" is a difficult challenge that grows easier as we begin to disengage from attachments and agendas that simply can't coexist with the discovery of God's will. Ignatius invites us to find the freedom God intended by choosing holy indifference as the way forward.

A Spiritual Direction Story
Vanthong Manivanh – Community Director

I am an Asian woman currently working for a non-profit, Urban Impact, whose main responsibility is to encourage local church involvement in serving at-risk youth and families in their community. Our mission is to break social, material, and spiritual poverty.

But I should back up. I grew up in Laos and my family came to the U.S. as refugees when I was in grade school. I came to Christ as result of a church that embraced my family in our transition. After completing college, I joined the Peace Corps and served in Madagascar for three years where I lived in a small village. In this isolated setting I was forced to nurture my relationship with God as a moment-by-moment experience of dependence.

Upon returning to the U.S., I intentionally looked for a spiritual director due to one fear: that the demands of life in the United States would suck me in and drown out the intimate connection with God that I had developed from ministering overseas for three years. In sharing the past eight years of my journey in a deep friendship through spiritual direction, I feel honored and blessed to have an amazing guide who helped me see who God created me to be and how I could lead out of who I am and the cross-cultural context in which I was raised.

With my spiritual director's help I was able to strengthen my intimacy with God. This helped me develop the habit of going before God for *every* aspect of my life. There were certain areas where I always went to God, and then there were others where I depended on my skills and social networks to find my way. Specifically, in my work with a spiritual director I discovered that I never consulted God about my career. This was an "ah-ha" moment for me.

This discovery had much to do with my cultural background and family traditions, which dictated where I should work. In my cultural tradition I felt obligated to honor my mom and family by rallying my resources and opportunities to assist them. (Choosing a career at Urban Impact was a financial step down.) Certainly my family value doesn't go against God, but it also meant I was not surrendering all of me, pouring out who I am for God's agenda.

When we surrender to God completely, we know there is freedom and blessing not only for us, but also for the body of Christ, and our community, including our families. Working with my spiritual director clarified God's voice. . . . I was compelled to completely give all of me to God. On this journey of surrendering to God, I rely on Jeremiah 42:3 which reminds me to "Pray that the Lord your [our] God will tell us where we should go and what we should do." My faith has grown. I feel I am more equipped for whatever life throws at me.

There are so many more examples of how my spiritual director has impacted my life that cannot be captured in these paragraphs. However, I will share one more with you. On this journey of intimacy with God, I also discovered that I am good and worthy of love. My background, what I do, or how I do it, does not define me. I love who I am now and I love who I will become because God has clearly stated I am his beloved. Out of that love I can love many others including my staff. Because of this lesson, I am a better leader, a leader who can walk beside her staff to discover who God created them to be. The hope is that they too will do the same for the people they supervise.

9

Going Deeper:
Contemporary Practices in Spiritual Direction

Janet Ruffing, who has written extensively on the practice of spiritual direction, uses a wonderful metaphor to describe this ministry:

> Spiritual direction is like panning for gold. A directee comes and together we dip into the stream for gold. . . . We dip into the stream of their life and pull up all kinds of things. Rocks of all sizes—I can never guess what's coming next—all kinds of conflicts and problems, then all of a sudden some fleck or nugget of pure gold emerges into view in the bottom of the pan as we swirl the water around, emptying out the rocks.[1]

Like someone who's learning to pan for gold, we need assistance to develop the art of spiritual direction. St. Ignatius has offered us a wonderful foundation. We now turn to contemporary writers and practitioners in this field to learn more about spiritual guidance. There are many questions to be asked: What does engagement in this ministry actually look like? What should a director do to lead the directee into paths of meaningful formation? Are there pitfalls that should be watched for and averted along the way? What is the difference between spiritual direction and counseling? What are the principle issues that present themselves when two people "pan for gold"?

To address these questions, I would like to highlight four topics that help to define the basic territory, and give practical insight into the process of spiritual direction. These are: 1) Listening to the Holy Spirit, 2) Listening to the directee, 3) The directee's view of God and self, and 4) The directee's prayer life. Each of these increases our understanding in both the receiving and giving of guidance.

Listening to the Holy Spirit

Central to all spiritual direction is the art of listening. Thomas H. Green envisions three parties in this process: "Director, directee, and the Holy Spirit, each one listening and learning from the conversation between the other two."[2] This is referred to as "three-fold listening." A spiritual director is someone who listens to the directee on behalf of God, and to God on behalf of the directee. And finally, the director needs to be listening to him or herself as they have an ear to God and the other. Let's begin by exploring what it means for the director to have an ear toward God.

Amid all of the material one can read in the field of spiritual direction, there is a primary theme that repeats itself: The Holy Spirit is truly the One who leads the process. The director's principal responsibility is to develop the art of dependence upon the Spirit. Francis Nemeck and Maries Coombs write, "As spiritual directors we operate first, foremost, and always from the premise that God is the only director of any person. We are consequently no more than God's instrument, albeit free instruments, in the process of spiritual direction."[3]

One of the greatest hindrances to spiritual direction is the tendency of the director to get in the way of the process. All too often, the director allows his or her own personality, feelings, and thoughts to fill the conversation. Of course, God intends to use the director, but not until he or she has assumed the proper place in the process. Jan Johnson emphasizes the humility involved in this practice. "To be a spiritual director is to give up being a 'star.' I'm only a facilitator watching the Holy Spirit work. My directees will know and love God without my expressing my brilliant insights."[4] For most of us, learning to listen for the voice of God is difficult, even foreign. It requires intentionality to stay out of the way and look to God as the one who leads the process.

Ignatius highlights this posture as one of a healthy "detachment." He counsels the director to ensure that the directee is able to do business with God and be free from any inappropriate interference from the director. Ignatius says, "So he who is giving the *Exercises* should not turn or incline to one side or the other, but standing in the center like a balance, leave the Creator to act immediately with the creature, and the creature with the Creator."[5] To "stand in the center like a balance" is to realize that acting as a director involves conscious reliance on God.

The choice to lead in ways that are healthily detached will involve an act of faith on the part of the director, one that defies the natural tendency to assume control. Control is our way of protecting ourselves and projecting our adequacy when we feel uncertain. Instead of listening we start to talk. However, spiritual direction is all about hanging on the edge of uncertainty and inadequacy. Francis Vanderwall makes this need for dependence very clear: "Qualified directors are those who are aware of their own incompetence to direct another in the awesome task of sacred work of leading another to God."[6]

Philip Sheldrake, an experienced retreat leader, expresses his sense of inadequacy: "In trying to come to terms with my fears over the years, the light has slowly dawned that in the retreat situation there is indeed a director, who is, however, not human but divine.

God is the director; I am a helper, the *giver* of the retreat."[7] The director must understand that to be truly present with the directee, he or she must also be obtrusively absent.[8]

Since listening to the Spirit requires a sensitive and patient posture, it will require discipline on the part of the director to slow the process down when necessary. In our wordy world, where silence is perceived as time wasted—or possibly even a demonstration of incompetence on the part of the director—there is the strong temptation to keep things moving. Nemeck and Coombs state:

> Instead of waiting to guide the directee when and as moved by the Holy Spirit, we easily let a myriad of human weaknesses get to us. For example, when the Spirit is silent we may feel obligated to say something out of desire for approval or as a misguided way of consoling an impatient directee. God may actually need our corresponding silence to bring about what he wants to accomplish in the directee.[9]

When we forget this fundamental truth, we stand to do more damage than good, for we operate from a place of human wisdom— even pride—as we seek to lead the way in and of ourselves.

A discipline must be learned. During the session, it is necessary to continually reorient oneself to the voice of God. Directors need to remind themselves of the reality that they are working in the midst of a mystery. Gerald May writes, "It is my belief that the primary task of spiritual directors is to encourage within themselves this moment-by-moment attention towards God as frequently as possible during the spiritual direction session."[10]

A further warning is in order if we desire to follow the pathway of healthy detachment. Since spiritual direction often involves processing emotional pain in the life of the directee, there is a tendency to feel the need to alleviate the stress and discomfort that surface in the session together. The director can easily rescue the situation by soothing the discomfort and rescuing the directee from disruption. This type of response not only harms the individual in need of direction by interfering with the action of God in the face of uneasiness and tension, it actually serves the director rather than the directee.

When "rescuing" occurs, the director has actually invaded the Holy Spirit's space in an attempt to inappropriately protect the individual. Leaders who are beginners in spiritual direction are especially prone to this type of pitfall. Many pastors have participated in a type of pastoral counseling over the years wherein they sought to help others by relieving their anxiety. Indeed, that was what was expected, so we dutifully fulfilled our role.

As a pilgrim in the art of learning spiritual direction, I have encountered the irresistible pull to steer away from dependence on the Holy Spirit. The magnetic draw to prove my capability as a leader comes from the false self I described earlier. I'm not alone. Many of us have an unhealthy obsession to be needed, appreciated, and affirmed.

This is a "dance" between three parties: director, directee, and Holy Spirit—one that requires a well-disciplined mind and heart on the part of the spiritual guide. An effective director will make it his or her goal to not only listen to the Holy Spirit himself, but also to teach the directee to be a listener. Most people who enter the process of guidance have never learned how to be attentive to the Holy Spirit's promptings. Gary Moon and David Benner emphasize the work involved in leading the directee into this state of personalized discernment rather than depending on the director to be the primary guide:

> The fundamental requirement for true spiritual direction
> is belief and trust that the Trinity is at work in the world

and in each of us *here and now*. The spiritual director helps the seeker to be attentive, open and responsive to the Spirit's presence and constant invitation to transformation. Spiritual direction helps us acquire a new way of seeing, of being aware, leading to a new way of personally responding to the self-communicating God.[11]

This journey into the knowledge of how to listen to the Holy Spirit as the primary guide is one that all spiritual directors struggle to learn. It is consoling to know that even those who are experienced guides must continually remind themselves of this truth. Rose Mary Dougherty is truly a seasoned director who offers her personal insight into the process of depending on God's Spirit:

> I have finally come to realize that while authentic spiritual direction has something to do with a sense of calling for those who participate in it, the real "success" in spiritual direction is not dependent upon my skills as a director. . . . Rather, the critical element of spiritual direction, which those involved share, is the intention to rely on God, to seek God actively and wait for God's leading. Where this can happen, between two individuals or within groups, hearts are opened, private agendas are put on hold and God's Spirit is given free rein.[12]

Listening to the Directee

Learning to listen to another person well is one of the most difficult tasks we face in life! We want so much to talk, to advise, to instruct. We have overlooked the transformative power of sacred listening. Someone has said, "Intense listening is indistinguishable from love, and love heals."[13] There are many schools of psychotherapy, but they have found that there is one healing principle that crosses all of them: *listening.*

Carl Jung, the great German psychiatrist states, "[E]veryone longs to tell his or her story to someone and have it understood and accepted."[14] Intentional listening is an art, one that is learned slowly, and not without many challenges along the way. It is also therapeutic in and of itself, for the directee comes to places of realization simply by articulating his or her own experience.

Fundamentally, directors are not listening to words and information; they are actually listening to sacred experience. It is through the drawing out of experiences that the director is able to lead the individual to join in the process of *panning for gold.* As we have already learned, there is no forward movement in our relationship with God without personal experiences from which to process his involvement in our lives. Similarly, there is no forward movement in spiritual direction unless this experience is shared and truly appreciated by the director. Listening is the only pathway to the place where both director and directee can process spiritual experiences together.

In order for directees to take possession of their experience, they must be able to express it for themselves. When the director functions as an attentive and creative listener, the door is opened to further movement in the heart of the directee. If the directee can make greater sense of the experience by articulating it, the person will be enabled "to discern the movements and the guidance of God in his (or her) life. He will be able to see the divine initiative of loving invitation, in which God is seeking from him some kind of response."[15] It is in formulating our experience in words that we are able to unravel the mystery that surrounds the events of our lives.

Therefore, nothing a director does is more important than being a listener for another person. To engage in this type of listening, one must develop the skill of asking questions, questions that lead into new places, deeper emotions, and personal discoveries. Margaret Guenther encourages this skill in her book, *Holy Listening: The Art of Spiritual Direction*:

A good teacher asks questions, but they must be the right questions—ones that open doors, invite the directee to stretch and grow . . . a gently asked question can be helpful to director and directee alike: "Could you say a little more about that? Can you give me an example of what you mean by . . .?"[16]

I remember the value of spiritual direction during my early stages of recovery following my slide into ministry burnout. I experienced an intense need to analyze why this leadership crisis entered my life as if finding an answer would fix it. I had always succeeded in all that I had done; this chapter in my life plan didn't fit. Many of the conversations with my director were an attempt to analyze the situation. My brain was on overdrive trying to make sense of something I had tried to avoid.

At one point, my spiritual director asked a penetrating question, one that has not left me to this day. This simple question reoriented everything: "Have you noticed how often you say 'I am trying to figure this out?'" My need to make sense of everything was my way of recovering control. If I could figure it out I could fix it, or at least ensure that it would never happen again. But, because the whole thing was beyond my control, I was at a loss to move on. My need for answers was holding me hostage.

When my director asked this question, I was stunned. No, I had not noticed how often I said the words "I'm trying to figure this out." But I certainly began to notice from that day forward. All of this has resulted in a deeper understanding of how I feel the need to process everything. Whenever there is tension, disappointment, or something that does not fit, I lock up in my mind. It turns into a mental challenge as I attempt to find answers to resolve the issue. My director's question caused me to reassess my basic assumptions about how life should work.

When spiritual directors are in a session, it is important to be alert to discern those statements that lead to fruitful discoveries. Guenther continues:

I am learning to notice statements that cry out for a clarifying question, especially when the directee encounters painful material or stands on the threshold of new awareness. Hints are dropped, bits of information are offered, and the narrative seems disjointed, almost as if the directee were saying, "I left a piece out there. What I am saying doesn't make sense. Why don't you ask me about it?"[17]

Of course, the value of asking questions is on display in the gospels. If we desire to learn the art of inquiry, we must study the master of spiritual direction. Jesus helped people move into their spiritual journeys by drawing out their true feelings, deepest desires, and internal inconsistencies in a way that encouraged growth. His questions often led to painful discoveries, ones that allowed the Spirit of God to convict, heal, and restore. Jean Laplace offers his experience as a director:

It is really possible to learn the art of asking questions, of getting someone to talk about the causes of his troubles, of which he is usually the last person to be aware, the art of breaking down the barriers, of helping to uncover the false motives that underlie his apparently most generous actions? And of discovering on the other hand the real inclinations of his being and the movements of the Holy Spirit.[18]

Listening, asking questions, and following the pathway toward what is real and true in the person's life will certainly involve risk. At the heart of spiritual direction is the courage needed to step into experiences that precipitate breakthroughs, which lead to disrupted places, unexpected emotion, and even more difficult work. Nemeck and Coombs state, "The basis for spiritual direction is complete abandonment to God in openness and receptivity. This act by its very nature necessitates the willingness to take risk."[19] They also suggest that "reluctance to risk can originate from a variety of sources: a desire for certitude and control, a lack of confidence, fear of making a mistake, pride, timidity, etc. The refusal to take risk stifles the spirit."[20]

The director must realize that vulnerability is mutual and felt at an even deeper level on the part of the directee. To reveal the truth about oneself is to take a terrific risk. In his book, *The Gift of Spiritual Direction*, Wilfrid Stinissen touches on the sense of fear and even the danger a directee feels when they tell the truth about themselves:

> Many feel ugly, dirty, miserable. When they finally get the courage—it takes courage to show your nakedness— and overcome their shame, it happens almost with trembling; Will my spiritual leader be shocked, will he still accept me when I speak the entire truth, will he break off all contact?[21]

In my own journey as someone under spiritual direction, I have often experienced a desire to skip my appointment out of a sense of shame. This shame is often precipitated by a perception, as I mentioned earlier, that my issues tend to be a needle that stays stuck on a scratched vinyl record—I repeat the same struggle over and over again simply surfacing it in a different way each time we meet. I remember beginning a conversation with my spiritual director once and stating, "I didn't want to come today. I feel like I am simply going to say the same things I said in my previous visits." I see the same pain in directees that come to see me. But wait— since when does life-change happen in one or two conversations?

Why wouldn't we expect to struggle for months and even years in the areas where our lives are marred and broken?

The listening ear of a wise soul friend, coupled with the gentle acceptance in the face of my embarrassment, is truly a gift. It is only when a director offers this gift that I am able to stay with my stuff, to press in, month after month and year after year. There is no progress when we abandon the process. The spiritual director holds the key that will allow the directee to walk into the real issues, ones that are attached to the fallen self. That key is the ability to listen well.

The Directee's View of God and Self

Much of what occurs in spiritual direction has to do with one's view of God and one's view of self. In this process of listening to the directee and to the Holy Spirit, the director must pay close attention as the directee's identity interfaces with his or her assumptions about God. A. W. Tozer has said, "What comes to our minds when we think about God is the most important thing about us."[22] In other words, when our view of God is skewed, everything that follows will be out of order. Therefore, the director has the daunting task of joining the process of being attentive to a person's deepest thoughts and feelings about how they view God and how they assume God views them.

When a directee is in conversation with the director, clues may surface indicating that an assumption regarding God is twisted, and this faulty assumption stifles progress in the directee's desire to know him. As was discussed previously, the director has the important task of dealing with the "double knowledge"— knowledge of God and knowledge of self. Effective spiritual directors will know how to move back and forth between these two places (view of self and view of God) to assist the directee toward spiritual health.

William Barry discusses the issues surrounding our view of God and self. He writes:

We also meet God with learned self-God schemata that derive from our relationships with parents and others, from teachings about God. . . . These schemata are always distorted and untrue to the reality of who God is for us. In other words, our experience of God is impoverished because of our self-God schemata. We could say that the development of the relationship with God consists in progressively learning more realistic images of self and God in relationship through the actual encounter with God.[23]

Many individuals who enter spiritual direction have made the assumption that God is disappointed in them. This is particularly true for people who come from a religious background where following God was often motivated by a sense of guilt and even shame. They were made to feel inadequate, and consequently never came to understand the genuine love and friendship of God toward them in spite of their deficiencies.

We might think that this faulty view of God is something Christian leaders don't struggle with. However, in my experience as a director, they frequently reveal their tendency toward a harsh view of God. According to Delcy Kuhlman, spiritual direction is "an environment in which one's image of God can be examined and can then soften as it grows to reflect love more accurately."[24]

The first goal of the Ignatian Exercises is designed to bring us face to face with our sin, but the deeper intention is to help the individual discover—even in the face of their sinfulness—that God accepts them unconditionally. Barry highlights how Ignatius sets out in this direction:

This affective principle and foundation can be called the experience of having a spiritual identity, a real relationship with God . . . without such an experience of God's primordial love and care, a person remains rooted in a distant, perhaps scrupulous, perhaps resentful, relationship with God.[25]

Obviously, this uncertainty about God leads toward a variety of issues. One that stands out is a resistance to prayer. In all relationships, if we have a sense that someone does not like us, then we have an aversion to being with them. Similarly, if we feel that God is disappointed in us, why would we feel comfortable spending time with him? Prayer becomes difficult and burdensome as we press into a relationship that only increases our sense of failure. "Such prayer becomes too painful to continue and we simply (and should not) enter into it anymore. We cannot endure prayer that leaves us always liking ourselves less."[26]

The starting point for recovery of a healthy view of God, one grounded in grace and not performance, will be the nature of the director's personal relationship with the directee. Through the process of spiritual direction, the director is able to "incarnate" the truth about God's grace, love, and unconditional acceptance.

When people discover that they can reveal all of their innermost struggles, disappointments, and sin, and still know that their director accepts them with a tender and welcoming heart, they can begin the journey toward believing that God feels the same way. Gerald Grosh states it succinctly: "The person's openness and trust of a director often precedes his openness and trust of the Lord."[27] This commitment to process the directee's view of God will take much time and insight. It is not possible to alter one's deepest assumptions without tracking them from many directions and always bringing them back to the truth that they are loved by God.

Joseph Tetlow highlights the director's objective for listening, clarifying, and examining the directee's longstanding and deeply embedded assumptions about God: "As you accept the true God as your God, you deepen your ability to accept yourself as you are—not as you might have been, or could have become, or ought to be. . . . You accept God's acceptance of you, and this brings with it a deep gratitude to God."[28]

In considering the importance of the directee's view of God and self, the director will ultimately deal with issues that are central to the field of professional counseling and therapy—personality, identity, self-esteem, broken relationships, etc. Hence, in the study of spiritual direction the question is often asked, "What is the difference between counseling and spiritual direction?" In his book *Spiritual Director, Spiritual Companion,* Tilden Edwards addresses this issue:

> Counseling is focused primarily on our emotional hang-ups—the ways we are limited in our capacity to cope with inner psychological forces with other people. . . . A divine force may be accepted in that relationship, but the primary intent of paying attention to that force is to use it to help us improve our personal effectiveness. In spiritual direction the focus is on that divine force, on God, as the integral core of our being and purpose. We go to a spiritual director because we want to become more attuned to God's Spirit in our spirit and freely live out of divine love, with the background help of scriptural interpretation and experiential spiritual tradition about what such love looks like.[29]

Since spiritual direction differs from counseling, the directee may need to be guided toward an understanding of what the process is like. Problem-solving easily becomes the primary focus in life. However, in time, the directee is able to see that the picture is bigger than their immediate concerns.

Len Sperry affirms, "Unlike psychotherapy . . . which focuses more on symptom reduction or problem resolution, spiritual direction focuses more on the maintenance and development of spiritual health and wellbeing . . . the basic goal of spiritual direction is to develop the directee's relationship with God."[30] While it is extremely helpful to have psychological insight, it is important to guard against believing that these skills are the foundation for spiritual direction. Some would even argue that the growing interest in spiritual direction is a result of the failure of therapy.[31] People are longing for more than resolution to their problems; they desire the meaning that is found in the mystery of knowing God while living into the questions life brings.

The Directee's Prayer Life

We have briefly mentioned that the directee's prayer life is a primary place to explore their view of God and self. Much more can be learned by giving careful consideration to the dynamics of prayer. Ignatius believed that processing one's experiences in prayer becomes a window into the person's relationship with God. He strongly advised spiritual directors to make the prayer life of the directee a focal point for discussion. Since prayer is the place where one's relationship with God occurs at the deepest level, it is important to carefully probe the dynamics that occur.

Marian Cowan and John Futrell highlight the director's responsibility when an individual receives spiritual direction during an Ignatian retreat. The essential content is what has been going on in his or her prayer life throughout the day: "joys, fears, consolation, desolation, strengthening of faith, hope, love, emptiness, aridity, distractions, attractions, calls apparently from God, gifted freedom, lack of freedom, peace, turmoil, presence or absence of God, and so on."[32] Most Protestants have no understanding of what it means to look into their prayer life this way. We rarely talk about our experiences in prayer—especially our negative experiences and disappointments.

At this point, it will be beneficial to contrast the Catholic and Protestant traditions. As we have noted previously, most of what we find in the field of spiritual direction is derived from the Catholic tradition that tends toward a more contemplative view of the spiritual experience. By "contemplative," we simply mean the individual relates to God in a more reflective or interior manner; they pause long enough to consider feelings, desires, and motives as well as God's presence in the midst of all that they experience.

It is this contemplative posture to prayer that is, to a large extent, missing in many Protestant ministries. The interior reflection that leads to union and communion with God is lost while focusing on the business and busyness of serving. At best, this leads to the development of a pragmatic view of prayer, which emphasizes the importance of activity and accomplishment, thereby keeping the focus on doing rather than being.

Many Christian leaders have a deep sense that their prayer life lacks true encounter with God. As a result, they have feelings of discouragement and even guilt or shame. A good spiritual director is aware that this disillusionment is actually a wonderful opportunity for spiritual formation. Dyckman and Carroll state:

> Sometimes what appears to be a blockage in prayer is rather a gift from God. Through darkness, aridity, and emptiness we are called to a new form of prayer . . . difficulty in prayer often marks the beginning of real prayer, prayer in which the Christian begins to seek, and to find not the consolations of God, but the God of consolations.[33]

The role of the spiritual director is to help the directee begin to process their prayer experiences in ways that lead to hope and new interest or hunger. They assist the individual in seeing how feelings of desolation (guilt, shame, perfectionism, self-effort, failure) have sabotaged their prayer life. Yet, there is something much deeper going on. According to Houdek, there is consolation:

> The alleged remoteness of God is actually the sign of a deepening relationship, an invitation to take the attention off oneself. It is also another example of the perennial invitation of God to self-surrender in trust. The person is being asked to simply surrender his or her control over prayer and the development of the relationship to the mysterious God of prayer.[34]

To enter into this deeper relationship with God, the director must help the directee get in touch with his or her deepest feelings. Unexpressed anger often exists when prayer is dry. When we feel relational dissonance, and choose not to express it to the other person, there is usually distance in that relationship. Barry and Connolly contend that "when such feelings are very strong, affective prayer is possible only if the person can put them before the Lord and let him accept them. Otherwise, the unnoticed negative feelings will stand like a ridge between him and the Holy One."[35] They add:

> The director will often find that the person does not readily express such feelings in prayer. He believes them to be unworthy . . . obstacles to be overcome so that worthy feelings can eventually be placed before the Lord. So he tries to ignore them, tries not to notice them. As a result, he has nothing to say to the Lord.[36]

Many leaders have come to the place where they "have nothing to say to the Lord"—nothing personal, nothing with feeling, nothing experiential. Roadblocks have sabotaged their friendship with God and they are prime targets for spiritual disillusionment. Spiritual direction—the kind that fosters the directee's courage to look closely at their prayer life, allowing them to express their frustration, doubt, boredom, and confusion with God—is desperately needed.

The late Henri Nouwen was asked by Kenneth Leech to write the introduction to his book, *Soul Friend*, and he chose to pen these words:

> Most simply expressed, spiritual direction is direction offered in the prayer life of the individual Christian. It is an art which helps discern the movements of the Holy Spirit in our life, assisting in the difficult task of obedience to these movements and offering support in the critical decisions that our faithfulness requires. Prayer, thus understood, embraces all of life, and spiritual direction is therefore a very awesome ministerial task.[37]

I trust that this chapter has helped you realize what an amazing gift soul friendship can be. Listening to God and the directee is an act of love. In so doing, we are able to discern the central issues that shape the directee's view of God and self and, as a result, impact his or her spiritual life. Taking this a step further, we learn even more as we carefully tend to the directee's view of God and their experience in prayer. These are the places where we will find wrong thinking and distorted ideas about God and are then able to nurture right thinking, leading to hope, change, and spiritual health. The leader's soul is formed.

In this sense, soul friendship is an art. The director learns to lead by creatively watching the thoughts that spill out in the conversation. He or she looks for entry points that are discerned in dependence on the Holy Spirit. Asking a question, or offering a word of wisdom, nurtures the directee's insights in their spiritual journey. The art of spiritual direction takes time. We learn to "paint" by getting into the mess and finding out what works and what does not. The director approaches their task with humility, realizing how much unknown territory there is to discover in the process of guiding others more effectively.

A Spiritual Direction Story
Dave Zollner – Former Bank Vice-President

Growing up in a large Catholic family in a small farming community, I was raised on the principle of hard work. I wanted to please my parents, so I earned a "good boy" reputation by serving as an altar boy at church, going to mass six times a week, and working hard at my chores on the farm. My dad was emotionally absent and used alcohol to cope with his own struggles; between working and drinking, there wasn't much space left in his life to be an involved father. I grew up with a vague sense that he loved me, but beyond that, he was basically uninvolved in my life.

Continuing my pattern of working to earn favor, in tenth grade I applied and was accepted to the nearby Benedictine seminary. I enrolled, but it quickly became clear that I was not emotionally or academically prepared for the rigors of monastic life. After less than a year, I left the seminary and returned to high school feeling deeply defeated and devalued.

What followed was more than four decades of that same work ethic repeating itself in most aspects of my life: military service, college education, marriage, career, fatherhood, community involvement, church leadership.

After parking my faith on a side street during my military and college years, I became a Christ-follower in my mid-twenties and began to pursue my faith in earnest. This took the form of study, learning, serving, and leading. In hindsight, it's clear that I approached spirituality through the lens of my personal work ethic, believing that if I worked hard and was persistent, God would approve of my efforts. Deep down, I believed that my performance would prove my worth. I figured God loved me, but was watching to see how I did in my faith pursuit; the jury was still out on whether or not he would fully affirm and approve of me.

At age fifty-eight, I left my professional life and began to pursue the question, "What are you going to do with the rest of your life?" Or as Gordon MacDonald asked in *The Life God Blesses*: "What kind of old man do you want to be?"

Soon I was reading a biography of St. Ignatius and developing an understanding of his journey in discernment of God's movements in his life. Through the encouragement of a soul friend, I was introduced to Bill, who became my spiritual director. Through years of practice, Bill had developed a keen ability to listen to the Holy Spirit, asking deeper questions and discerning small movements of God. Our monthly meetings were like a door being opened to my soul.

Bill's thoughtful questions and listening helped me realize that after growing up with an emotionally absent dad, I had unknowingly put my heavenly Father into the same category—labeled "not here, not interested." As I began to explore my relationship with my heavenly Father, I realized I didn't have a clear sense of his presence. I experienced Jesus and the Holy Spirit as real and involved in my life, but the idea of being in relationship with "Abba Father," a loving daddy? It was a foreign concept.

A breakthrough came during a retreat at the same abbey where I had briefly attended seminary as a young student almost fifty years earlier. Pondering the patterns of my life, I began to see for the first time that for many years, God had been putting men in my life to mentor me in unique ways. One friend asked, "Is it possible that God has been expressing his love to you through the mentors he has been putting in your life?" I began to see God's fingerprints all over my life.

One evening at the abbey I lay in my bed with the lights off, eyes open, tears streaming down my cheeks and saying out loud, "Daddy, Abba! Where have you been? Why haven't you been in my life? I don't know you!" Only a brief moment passed before I heard the voice in my heart say, *I have been here all the time, but you haven't been ready to let me in.* I sobbed in the newfound awareness that far from being an unavailable and uninvolved father figure, God had been there all along . . . that my Father did love me and wanted to be intimately involved in my life.

10

Restoring Spiritual Direction in Today's World

We have reached the last chapter in our journey toward a deeper understanding of spiritual direction. To finish well we need to shift our trajectory. While I trust everything written to this point has had practical implications in your life, this chapter is designed to move toward application at a deeper level. You may be asking, "If spiritual direction is a critical exercise in the life of the leader, how do I get from here to there?" Most Christian leaders have had little or no exposure to this type of ministry in their lives. At the outset of this book I indicated we would work toward two outcomes:

First, I suggested that you might want to look for a trained spiritual director—someone who has learned the art through study and one-to-one experience. My goal in this chapter will be to assist you in knowing how to seek out the right person as a spiritual director, someone who will function as a soul friend to you as a leader.

Second, I indicated you might want to consider something called "group spiritual direction" (group means as few as two and not more than five or six). This type of direction is not complicated to implement and yet profoundly transformational. My goal will be to help you understand the nature of group spiritual direction and offer guidance to initiate this type of experience.

It's time to tackle these two outcomes. As I do, I would like to invite you to prayerfully consider if spiritual direction should be part of your life, either by seeking out a personal director or by birthing a group that shares in this experience together. I believe this practice is foundational when it comes to maintaining spiritual health in the challenging, and often overwhelming, world of leading people and organizations. *If it's sustainable and joyful ministry we desire, then spiritual direction is a fundamental step toward fostering this outcome. The leader's soul must be formed, and so I offer you an invitation to spiritual direction.*

FIRST: Guidance for Those Who Seek a Spiritual Director

Many leaders in the Protestant tradition are just now becoming aware of spiritual direction. Even though it may look like an appealing spiritual rhythm, they feel a high degree of uncertainty when it comes to getting started. For most leaders, seeking out a spiritual director seems rather daunting since this practice is foreign to their spiritual journey. Many of us don't know how to navigate this new territory, and as a result we remain stalled. Help is needed if we hope to make the move toward finding a spiritual director.

When my wife and I moved to a different city, I was forced to search for a new spiritual director. I remember stumbling around for months with feelings of uncertainty about how to find the right person. It would have been easy to give up, yet I knew I had to push through my hesitancy. I can't tell you how important the decision to press ahead proved to be. God brought the right person to my mind and into my life. We meet monthly. Together with my director I have processed critical issues related to my view of God, forgiving others, and feelings of spiritual disillusionment.

Let's walk through the steps that must be addressed by someone who is searching for a spiritual director. To begin with, you should have a good grasp of the characteristics that make up a mature and effective soul friend. To whom should someone entrust himself or herself? This is a question of paramount importance to the individual who desires a director. No one would consider choosing a mountain climbing guide without having full confidence that this person has traveled the terrain many times and carries with him or her not only the knowledge but also the necessary equipment for a safe climb. How much more care should be given to the selection of a spiritual guide? So what are we looking for? Let's answer that question.

Qualifications of a Director

There are many qualifications that might be considered when seeking a spiritual guide. However, when all the possibilities are distilled, there are only a few characteristics that are absolutely essential:

1. *Spiritual Discernment:*

- Does this person demonstrate wisdom in matters of the spiritual life when you talk with them? Do they connect spiritual truth with everyday reality?

- Has this person earned the respect of other spiritual leaders?

2. *Listening and Asking:*

- Does the director demonstrate highly tuned listening skills? Soul friends listen well and with empathy. Additionally, do you sense they know how to listen to God on your behalf?

- Since asking good questions is at the heart of transformative spiritual direction, do they demonstrate this skill? Do their questions help you discover new avenues where Christ is present in your life?

3. *Biblical Understanding:*

- Does the person have a strong grasp of the scripture and theology, and do they know when and how to integrate God's truth into the discussion?

- Is their theology *relational* in nature, meaning, are they able to apply the truth of God's Word to your life in an experiential way?

4. *Objectivity:*

- Will this person "speak the truth in love" with you (Ephesians 4:15)? Will they be tender, yet frank, in their conversation? Wilfrid Stinissen writes, "To harmonize tenderness and strength in relation to the confidant is one of the guide's most difficult tasks."[1]

- Is this person able to live with your unresolved difficulties, or do they demonstrate a need to "fix" you? As we have learned, the director must be able to live in the tension of an "unfinished life." The director reflects Paul's conviction: "It is God who is at work in you to act in order to fulfill his good purpose" (Philippians 2:13).

5. *Trust and Confidentiality:*

- Do you feel safe sharing your deepest thoughts, feelings, concerns, and problems with this person?

- Does this person have a track record of honoring people's confidences? Thomas Green states, "Spiritual direction, like the sacrament of reconciliation, requires strict confidentiality. The person being directed shares his inner self, his most personal possession. It belongs exclusively to him."[2]

6. *Compatibility:*

- When I am with this person, am I able to relax and express my deepest thoughts and concerns freely?

- Does this person respond to me in a way that connects? Does their temperament and way of relating foster confidence?

To determine compatibility, a directee may need to spend one or two sessions with a potential director before they will have a sense of whether this person "fits" or not. Sometimes it is necessary to move to another director if it becomes obvious that working together is leading to disappointment and even frustration. Working with your spiritual director should be engaging and life-giving.

Choosing a Director

At the heart of choosing a spiritual director is a commitment to prayer filled discernment. Seeking a spiritual guide requires trust in God. It is of utmost importance to stop and realize that God desires to guide you to a soul friend. For this reason, prayer and discernment are the starting points as you begin the journey of seeking the right person. Invite the Spirit to bring the individual of his choice across your path—a person who gives you a sense of inward confirmation and a desire to meet and discuss the possibility of working together.

It took me about six months to find the spiritual director I am now working with. I kept scanning the horizon for people who might fit. Various individuals crossed my mind, but I finally settled on a former pastoral colleague—someone I had known for many years. It didn't take long until I knew the chemistry was conducive to deep spiritual conversation, and our relationship of spiritual direction has grown over the months and years. In the search for a spiritual director, it is wise to network with people who already have one. It is not uncommon to find our way to the right person through people who are already in process.

Another avenue of seeking a guide would be to contact organizations and educational institutions that specialize in the training of directors. You may also want to check with retreat centers that offer spiritual direction as part of their ministry. It will take time and prayerful attention to find possible directors and then discern the right person, someone who demonstrates the qualities, approach, and temperament that give you a sense of confidence. Many leaders are too busy to take this journey. However, in the end, a high price is paid for neglecting such a treasured friendship.

The qualifications listed above might raise a question. Should a director be trained or certified, or could they be qualified through life experience rather than official education? The answer to this question is open-ended. First of all, training in spiritual direction is a wonderful asset. There is much to learn about the spiritual care of others, and to be both gifted of God and trained is a strong combination. When the director has training it can give the directee a sense of confidence, knowing that the necessary knowledge and skills have been nurtured.

However, and more importantly, spiritual direction is a gift—a *charism* of the Holy Spirit. Certain people simply demonstrate the qualities that attract others for guidance. *When it comes to choosing a spiritual director, this is far more important than any official training.* Such people have the gift of wisdom, and through years of relational experience, qualify to guide others. I know of various spiritual directors who are highly respected, yet they were never officially certified.

I would encourage the directee to interview the person whom they think could function as their director. Such a discussion will help to clarify if the fit seems right. Additionally, if someone has entered into direction and feels the director is not compatible, it is appropriate to end the commitment. Sometimes we need the courage to move on. However, this requires prayerful discernment. There are seasons when spiritual direction can be difficult and unsettling. Caution is needed. Discernment must be exercised so that, if a change is made, it is done so for healthy reasons.

In the history of the church we are given serious counsel regarding this matter of choosing a director. William of Saint-Therry (1085–1148) offers this: "If you accept my counsel, you will select for yourself a man whose life is such that it will act as a personal model to touch your heart, one whom you respect so much that whenever you think of him you will keep going because of the esteem you have for him."[3] Saint John of the Cross (1542–1591) warns that the individual must pay careful attention "to the hands in which it entrusts itself, for as the teacher is, so will the pupil be."[4] Charles de Foucauld (1815–1916) adds his counsel: "Before choosing their director, the brothers and sisters will pray fervently to God to guide their choice, then they will choose with maturity, reflection and serious consideration."[5]

On the other hand, when choosing a spiritual director, one must also be careful to guard against the possibility of placing the bar too high. We can feel paralyzed in our pursuit of a director if we start with a set of unrealistic expectations so that no one qualifies. Certainly God has surrounded us with people we respect, whose hearts are tuned to God, and who have our best interests in mind even as they struggle on their journeys.

In the end, we must choose someone, though they are imperfect, or we will abandon the process of spiritual direction before we begin. After prayerful preparation, we must step out and ask for help. I like Eugene Peterson's honesty when he finally found the "right" person in his search for a soul friend:

> I met a man whom I gradually came to feel was the right person. The more I knew him, the more confident

I became that he would understand me and guide me wisely.

At this point I greatly surprised myself: I didn't ask him. I was convinced I needed a spiritual director. I was reasonably sure this person would help me. And suddenly I felt this great reluctance to approach him. We were together quite regularly, and so I had frequent opportunities to approach him. I procrastinated.

It didn't take me long to get to the root of my reluctance: I didn't want to share what was most essential to me. I wanted to keep control. I wanted to be boss. . . . I wanted to be in charge of my inner life. I wanted to have the final say-so in my relationship with God.[6]

We need to step out believing there is a right person. And when we find them we need to ask.

Qualifications of a Directee

Having outlined the qualifications for seeking a spiritual director I also want to add some expectations that rest on the directee. The individual seeking guidance must demonstrate openness to God and a sincere desire for the truth—truth about themselves. The person must have a passion to discern God's will, transcend personal preferences for the sake of growth, and overcome obstacles along the way. They must be willing to develop awareness of self by tending to their internal workings, longings, and questions that go on within.

Growth in self-awareness is truly the only "material" a director has to work with. Unless the individual presents something meaningful, the director has nothing with which to "pan for gold." Francis Nemeck and Marie Coombs state, "Directees have to be able to reveal the secret aspirations which they cherish in their hearts, since their hearts are the secret refuge to which they can escape."[7] When a person enters into spiritual direction they must be willing to grow in ways that will feel painful at times. Facing the false self involves a type of surgery, and it takes courage to tell the "doctor" the symptoms of our sickness.

As I shared earlier, in my own journey I came to realize that much of my ministry as a pastor was motivated by the need for affirmation. It came as a shock to me when God exposed the motivations driven by my false self. Facing my narcissistic tendencies of leadership induced grief and sorrow. I had to come out of denial to receive the truth about myself before I could grow into freedom. Self-awareness was critical, and only people who have invited God to engage at this level will find spiritual direction meaningful.

When both director and directee converge with right motives and qualifications, the possibilities for spiritual formation are exciting. The seeking individual will have found a new source for nurture, one that will open windows in their journey toward God. James Houston describes these possibilities:

> A spiritual friend is someone with whom it is safe to take apart our shallow faith, our compulsive addictions, or whatever else might be under the surface of our visible lives. He or she will help us to exchange our weaknesses for a new source of trust, conviction, and desire to help us grow spiritually. We have been born into and grown up in a culture which is deeply alienated from God. So as we cross the border into God's kingdom, with its radically new attitudes and priorities, we will need all the help we can get from a spiritual friend who has made the same perilous journey before.[8]

Finally, there is one more principle the directee must understand when entering spiritual direction: This journey requires a long-term commitment. The discoveries to be made will come to light through various conversations. Consistency is the key. Kevin Barry has said, "Eighty-percent of all success here is you have to keep showing up for direction."[9]

In my personal life, I have discovered there are many times I simply do not want to follow through with my next direction appointment. Sometimes I go feeling uncertain about what needs to be discussed. At other times, I know what needs attention, but I don't want to admit it again. Yet, I keep on going. And, I can wholeheartedly affirm Barry's advice: "Eighty-percent of success is just showing up."

Most spiritual directors meet monthly with their directees, but there is no official pattern, and scheduling is something that both parties must work out according to their particular circumstances. I should also mention that there are times when face-to-face appointments are not possible. Personally, I do a considerable amount of spiritual direction by phone and over the internet. Overseas workers are now able to connect with a spiritual director as a result of the technological realities of our world.

SECOND: Guidance for Those Seeking Group Spiritual Direction

About ten years ago, I entered into group spiritual direction by "accident." Before I even knew what spiritual direction was, I chose two close friends and leaders in our church, and we began to meet weekly to process our spiritual journeys. This wasn't a bible study—we were all thoroughly grounded in the scriptures. This was an attempt at "soul talk" as we endeavored to be leaders who were seeking to be formed. We sought to integrate the truth into our everyday life. We longed for transformation at the deepest level of our thoughts and emotions. Each week we started with one person sharing, and when we felt like we had covered all the territory, we moved on. It was intensely relational and vulnerable. There were no secrets. We shared our sin, our sorrow, and our "success." Chuck and Joel became my soul friends. Without realizing it, we had entered "group spiritual direction."

My next learning experience in the value of group spiritual direction came as a result of attending a ten-day training experience where a gifted director offered instruction. We were placed in groups of three and carefully led to practice the principles that ensured we would stay on target. Without good structure and a solid understanding of the art of spiritual direction, it is easy for groups to cave into nothing more than extended coffee shop chats. However, when proper practices are secured—and honored with intentionality—group spiritual direction holds unusual potential to be formative at the deepest level of a leader's soul.

As my ministry journey continued, I believed God was leading me to focus on the spiritual and emotional health of other leaders. I was also completing my doctorate in Leadership and Spiritual Formation at George Fox University and was deeply engaged in further study of spiritual direction. At this time, I followed my dream and, with the support of some amazing friends, founded SoulFormation as a nonprofit organization designed to nurture the spiritual and emotional health of leaders. As SoulFormation grew, a driving question kept roaming through my mind: "How could we help more leaders learn the art of spiritual direction?"

I came to believe that if we connected leaders in the context of group spiritual direction, we could guard one another from the emotional and spiritual isolation that sabotages so many. Spiritual direction had become so meaningful for me that I was now looking for ways to lead others to this life-changing experience. I could also see that certain people were gifted to offer this type of care, but they had never been asked or trained to include direction as part of their calling. At this point, other leaders who shared the same vision joined me and together we committed to engage in group spiritual direction. We began to encourage and train others who longed for these kinds of transformational groups.

Much of our working strategy for training others in group spiritual direction is taken from Alice Fryling's book, *Seeking God Together: An Introduction to Group Spiritual Direction.* If group spiritual direction seems like a good fit for you, I would strongly encourage you to make this your guidebook. She offers this definition:

> Group spiritual direction is very similar to individual spiritual direction. A small group of people meet together to provide spiritual direction to each other. Members of the group are given the opportunity, one at a time, to be the directee, and the group responds prayerfully to whatever the directee chooses to present.[10]

One unique thing about group spiritual direction is that it does not require a trained spiritual director. Together we rely on the Holy Spirit and the collective wisdom of the group. Keeping the cluster small (five to six people maximum), along with regular attendance, are central components to the effectiveness of this approach. If it is a group of two, then one functions as the directee for the first half of the time together, after which the roles shift.

Most leaders have been involved in various types of small group experiences. However, group spiritual direction is unique and requires an approach that differs significantly from other small group formats. I would encourage leaders who choose to birth a group to also engage in the study of the basic principles and practices offered by mature spiritual directors who have written on this subject. These guides, whether ancient or contemporary, have much to offer as we seek to avoid the pitfalls and strengthen the quality of group work. The more we learn, the more we are able to participate at a deeper level. With basic guidance from those who are skilled, we can start a journey into group spiritual direction. I include a recommended reading list at the end of this book.

The Practice of Group Spiritual Direction

In her book, Alice Fryling outlines the framework for a group meeting. I would like to highlight a modified version of her template for you. Over time, I have discovered that honoring the flow and timeline Fryling offers is critical. It doesn't take much to throw a group off track. (One spiritual director told me that extroverts could talk for half an hour and think it is only ten minutes. Meanwhile, introverts talk for ten minutes and, to them, it feels like half an hour.) There is great wisdom in holding carefully to time frames like the following:[11]

Brief check-in: *5 minutes*
Each member shares a short update

Opening time of quiet: *5 minutes*
Possibilities for this time include:
- Silence
- Quiet music
- Guided meditation, scripture or spiritual reading

Group spiritual direction: *30–40 minutes for each person*
Directee presents – *15 minutes*
Time of silence – *2 minutes*
Group responds and interacts with directee – *15 minutes*
Time of silent prayer for directee – *2 minutes*
Time for the directee to debrief how the experience felt – *1 minute*

If the group has more than three participants, you may need to adjust the schedule to suit the dynamics. Spiritual direction must not feel rushed. An alternative would be to meet more frequently, focusing on two or three people each time and then shifting to the other members at the next meeting.

Throughout the chapters of this book I have covered some

critical themes that characterize what would take place in individual spiritual direction. So much of what I have written is foundational for the practice of group spiritual direction. If you choose to foster a group I encourage you to process these themes and then apply them to the context of group spiritual direction:

- Sacred listening—to the other person and to the Holy Spirit
- Asking good questions that open doors of discovery
- Gently probing motivation and exposing the false self
- Exploring inner experiences of consolation and desolation
- Engaging in discernment to recognize where Christ is present
- Using the scriptures with imagination to encounter Christ
- Aligning our decision-making process with God—"holy indifference"
- Exploring our desires to discover how God is prompting us
- Examining (and realigning) our view of self and God
- Processing the truth about our experience in prayer

I think of spiritual direction (either individual or group) as a place of "verbal journaling." Talking helps us think and reflect in a unique way. When we hear ourselves expressing something in the presence of others, it takes on a new light. Fresh thoughts surface as we share. We ask ourselves, *Do I really believe this? Why am I expressing this with such intensity? How does this connect with that (another feeling or thought)? What is underneath this emotion? Am I avoiding something? Why?*

Over the years I have had the privilege of visiting various group experiences as an observer and guide. From what I have learned, I would offer the following advice. First, it is critical to appoint a facilitator and encourage this person to adhere to the pattern that has been outlined. Without a good facilitator the group deteriorates into something less than it could be. Remember to share the facilitating responsibilities from week to week so that each person learns how to carry out this important role. It is good to use a timer to help people stay on track. This may seem stiff at first, but once you discover the flow it will feel natural and bring a sense of freedom knowing that structure is in place. I am in a group that has been meeting for years and we still use a timer. It allows us to focus.

Second, it is essential that each person bring something of personal significance to share with the group. This requires advance preparation. The directee must ask himself or herself, "What primary theme has become apparent in my life where discernment is needed? How can I best articulate this issue when my time comes to present?" It is easy to be self-protecting and fail to take the time to necessary to uncover the areas where one is experiencing *consolation* or *desolation*. I would encourage you to go online and Google "list of emotions"—print them out and keep them in your Bible or journal. Look them over carefully and pay attention to those emotions that have been dominating your experience. Our emotions are often the place where we discover clues to the areas that need attention: Am I anxious, fearful, hopeful, encouraged, depressed, confused, and so on? Ask yourself, "What is this emotion revealing or asking of me?"

Third, spiritual direction is built around intentional listening and asking good questions. This is the area where most groups slip—we so desperately want to give advice. And, yes, there are times when it is extremely helpful to offer a word of wisdom. However, when someone falls into the trap of being an advice giver, it is best for the facilitator to suggest restating his or her thoughts in the form of a question. Our goal is to help the directee do her or his own spiritual work. There are times when a group will feel stuck—no one will know what to ask. *This is the when someone should suggest that everyone stop for a minute or two of silence.* Sit quietly together as you listen to the Holy Spirit. Doing so will reveal the next turn in the road. At first it will feel a bit awkward, but the outcome is often a powerful question that leads to a breakthrough.

As you learn to function as effective spiritual guides for one another, the potential for increased awareness and spiritual discoveries are significantly enhanced. Directees will find themselves saying, "I never knew this about myself. I think I can see how God might be present in all of this." What a gift to have the collective wisdom of the group to help us gain insights we would never have known. Doing good work with soul friends is life-giving!

A word of warning is in order: Whenever leaders get together, it is extremely easy to allow the conversation to turn into shoptalk— we want to chat about our ministry experiences. This often leads to comparison that closes down the possibility of authenticity . . . we have egos to defend. Spiritual direction must move deeper. We are seeking to present aspects of our lives where help is needed in determining how God is present and how we are being formed. If we get caught up in discussing our careers, the facilitator should call the group back to the vital work of spiritual direction. The conversation must be redirected – there are many good questions that, once asked, will take the group *below the water line*!

In conclusion, I want to encourage each reader to seriously consider group spiritual direction because it holds something every Christian leader needs—a place where others listen to our soul and shepherd us at the deepest level. When we are able process the highs and lows of life together we discover how Christ is making himself known. There is newfound hope as we discover freedom and joy even in midst of difficulty and pain. We have soul friends and our experiences together are sacred.

Making Sustainable Ministry a Reality

We have come to an end of this examination of the world of spiritual direction. As we do, I would return us to our starting point: Leaders are at risk on a spiritual and emotional level. The critical component to help them is not further training in ministry development skills. The culture of the church has been fixated here long enough, circling around one primary goal: How do we get results? We do not need more conferences, training events, and "how to" books to move us forward!

What is desperately needed is a deeper commitment, one that is much harder to nurture and not easily measured. The central focus must become the formation of leaders through the development of "relational models" of spiritual formation. Roy Oswald of the Alban Institute shares this concern. He warns that even though ministry is our business, "staying healthy spiritually remains a significant challenge for clergy. We're supposed to be experts on spiritual matters, but we get little support for taking regular time to feed our spiritual hunger."[12] A commitment to the nurturing of the leader's spiritual health is the missing component in most churches and Christian organizations.

In the history of the church, pastors were referred to as "doctors or physicians of the soul." I like that analogy. A person's soul can succumb to all kinds of disease. They need specialized help to diagnose the symptoms and regain health.

Some time ago, I visited a friend in the hospital. I decided to stop in the cafeteria for lunch. As I sat down next to the windows, I observed something that left me feeling confused. Standing outside were a number of medical professionals, dressed in hospital attire, who were smoking. I simply could not connect the dots. I was looking at people who treat others with cancer and heart or respiratory diseases caused by smoking, while at the same time they were damaging their own health.

Not long after, I thought about the world of pastors and Christian leaders and it hit me: We are "doctors of the soul," who make the same fatal error. While tending to the spiritual condition of others, we knowingly overlook our own health. We allow ourselves to engage in practices that are destructive and avoid practices that are health-giving. Often, the very settings in which we work encourage and perpetuate patterns that result in sickness of the soul. As leaders we succumb to habits that function at cross-purposes to the nurture of our own spiritual well-being.

The time has come to face the realities of ministry and leadership with an honest assessment and a strategy for wellness. Spiritual direction is a proven pathway to health, and we are in need of leaders who understand the urgency of this ministry—women and men who will seek to reverse the course of events in their own lives and the lives of their colleagues in ministry. David Benner says it so well:

> My great hope is that those of us who long for a deeper experience of God would accept no substitute until this hunger is fulfilled. For us, spiritual direction holds great promise. It offers us a relationship of accountability within which we can walk the Christian path with another Christian. It offers us a place within which we can know ourselves as we are truly known. It offers us a place to meet God.[13]

In the years ahead, I expect we will see the interest in spiritual direction surging. Those who genuinely care should address this increased interest by using their influence to shape the future of spiritual formation in our churches and organizations. For years leaders have languished under a paradigm that often leads to emotional and spiritual disorder. "We have met the enemy and he is us."

In our search for a way out, I believe fresh winds are blowing.

We are poised to rediscover the ministry of spiritual direction—and with it, a new world of relational spiritual formation and personal growth that leads to sustainable ministry practices. *Forming the leader's soul must become our first priority if we hope to do God's work God's way.*

A Spiritual Direction Story
Arlene Weigand – A Pastor

It is not the fear of forgetting when the world seems to scream "Do Not Forget" in reference to September 11, 2001. For me, it is the all too present reality of what I remember and how this one day propelled me on a journey that would lead to discovering the unfathomable value of spiritual direction.

I am an ordained elder and was serving as senior pastor of a church in Brooklyn, New York, on 9/11/01.

- I remember when the first plane hit and running to watch it all unfold from the sanctuary windows.

- I remember the sounds of sirens, which to this day still cause a little sense of panic to rise within me.

- I remember standing outside in front of the church with the ash falling like a first snowfall and a momentary sense of peace—until one of the kids on the block asked me if I thought the ash was the ashes of the dead people.

- I remember being in shock for days and weeks and months. Trying to go forward with life, but feeling a gaping hole . . . literally where the towers had stood and figuratively where there was a void of knowledge—no answers, no explanation, no understandings.

- I remember feeling lost—in my faith, in my leadership, in who I was.

- I remember passion without joy and passion without purpose.

- I remember having a desperate longing for God to show up in glory and only facing the same pain and grief and despair each day.

- I remember beginning a sabbatical leave and being broken emotionally, physically, and spiritually—absolutely fractured.

- I remember the months of counseling and healing to restore my physical and emotional self.

You see, I remember 9/11 and the sadness continues to be deep within me. It wasn't until a decade later that I sat in the safety of God's presence with my spiritual director, and then in a spiritual direction triad, that my soul began to heal.

My group spiritual direction experience began with two friends who were on their own journeys toward renewal. In one of our earliest sessions together, I came thinking I had nothing to share. But, after sitting in silence before God suddenly all of the emotion and anger and fear I was holding onto from that one day started spewing out in sobs and anger and questions I had not been able to express or voice before.

I expected my friends to offer the same words I had heard from the world for the past ten years. But instead, they sat silently, in prayer, in tears, and allowed God to meet me and speak to me. In this sacred place I felt safe for the first time to tell some of the story—not to them, but to God.

I remember how God met me on this day and how I rediscovered His sovereignty blended with a deep compassionate love.

I remember that: "My God is my rock, in whom I take refuge, my shield and the horn of my salvation, my stronghold. . . . He reached down from on high and took hold of me; he drew me out of deep waters. He rescued me from my powerful enemy, from my foes, who were too strong for me. They confronted me in the day of my disaster, but the LORD was my support. He brought me out into a spacious place; he rescued me because he delighted in me" (Psalm 18:2, 16–19).

Appendix:
A Message for Presidents and Executive Leaders of Denominations, Colleges, and Christian Organizations

If we hope to forge a recovery of spiritual direction throughout the world of Christian leaders, we will need individuals to champion the cause at the highest levels of influence. Most denominational and parachurch executives in the Protestant tradition have little or no understanding of the ministry of spiritual direction.

A primary intent of this book has been to raise awareness among those who oversee others to a level of understanding that results in the advance of spiritual direction. Most organizational leaders know that ministers under their care are struggling with issues of emotional and spiritual heath—issues that impact their effectiveness and sustainability over the long haul.

The sad truth is that in many circles of religious leadership, we allow for the "commodification" of Christians leaders to occur. They are seen for what they can do and not for who they are. As the years pass, many pastors and leaders slip into embitterment, realizing that their giftedness was used to advance organizational purposes rather than advance the kingdom of God. They lost track of their souls amid all the career demands and affirmation.

If denominational and organizational leaders are reading the signs of the times, they are well aware that strategies for spiritual formation are desperately needed. It is my belief that spiritual direction, if properly introduced and nurtured, represents one of the critical pieces in the strategic move toward health. The question that always arises at this point is simple: Where do we turn for spiritual direction? Who is gifted and trained to offer the ministry of soul friendship to Christian leaders?

Gerald May highlights the fact that although people are rediscovering the value of traditional spiritual direction, "they have found the church ill-prepared. Protestants have almost no tested and accepted methods of individual spiritual direction."[1] To reverse this trend, leaders who oversee others might want to consider these steps:

1. **Become a directee yourself**: Key leaders must influence by modeling what it is they desire for others. It is impossible to take someone to a place where you have never journeyed. For this reason, Eugene Peterson, Leighton Ford, Ruth Barton, Richard Foster, Larry Crabb, and other respected leaders in the evangelical world have given a united call for leaders to take the voyage into spiritual direction. Organizational executives must follow this advice if they hope to establish this vital ministry in the lives of those under their care. In our world of "doing" we often excuse ourselves from the very practices that we know are necessary for spiritual health.

Life is busy. Yet, Ignatius may have put his finger on many key leaders when he raises the issue of "inordinate attachments." Could it be that most executives lack the awareness needed to see the way in which their work has become their identity and, in the end, is actually sabotaging the kind of union God desires? The discipline of spiritual direction allows for space to reorient around kingdom goals and help others do the same.

As you think about spiritual direction, remember the two avenues highlighted in the previous chapter: You could seek out a spiritual director and meet one-to-one, or you could find a handful of people who will commit to group spiritual direction together.

2. **Locate directors and training programs**: Denominational and organizational leaders can choose to locate spiritual directors who already meet the qualifications listed in the previous chapter. Those who have training and experience could be offered to leaders who are seeking help. I have found that there are numerous people hidden within the body of Christ who are ready to offer this type of care to others. Finding them takes some initiative, but they are quietly carrying out their ministry, realizing that self-promotion is not congruent with the ministry of spiritual direction. Encouraging one's staff to connect with people who are gifted and called to this ministry is necessary.

Also, there are numerous training programs that have sprung up across the country as awareness has grown. Leaders of churches, denominations, and organizations should make themselves aware of such training opportunities and seek out potential directors from within their sphere of influence—people they feel should be trained and encouraged to care for others. We need to foster the gift of direction from within our circles as we discover leaders who are capable of soul care. If we hope to recover spiritual direction in today's church, there must be a concerted effort to train individuals toward this end. When Henri Nouwen addressed the challenge of the scarcity of spiritual directors, he offered this encouragement:

> Spiritual guides are hard to find. This might be true, but at least part of the reason for this lack of spiritual guides is that we ourselves do not appeal to our fellow human beings in such a way as to invite them to become spiritual leaders. . . . There are many men and women with great spiritual sensitivity whose talents remain dormant because we don't make an appeal to them.[2]

Stephen Macchia highlights the critical importance of raising up directors within the body of Christ:

> If a new outpouring of spiritual wisdom is to come upon God's church, then pastors and leaders in positions of spiritual authority must be prepared. If spiritual formation and direction are to be experienced in local churches, then servant leaders must be raised up who have demonstrated their ability to serve as spiritual guides.[3]

3. **Rethink seminary training**: One of the key recommendations to further spiritual direction is made by Forster Freeman, who has done significant research on the issue of spiritual direction within the seminary experience. He writes:

> When an Alban Institute research team surveyed clergy who had been in a parish for up to three years, they uncovered a gaping hole in their seminary preparation. These recently ordained clergy repeatedly complained that they had little awareness of their own spirituality.[4]

For too long the seminary world has focused on theological information and pragmatic skill development. Little attention is given to the spiritual life of the student. Realizing this, Freeman tested his hypothesis: "Students in protestant seminaries would benefit more from their education for service in the church and work when that training included specific assistance with their personal spiritual formation."[5]

In his book, *Readiness for Ministry Through Spiritual Direction*, Freeman outlines case studies of various students who were chosen for spiritual direction while in seminary. The results confirmed (as we would expect): Students who were engaged in spiritual direction felt better prepared for ministry following their seminary training. Furthermore, if we introduce students to the ministry of spiritual direction in college, it would build relational spiritual formation into the fabric of their ministry.

Unless we give attention to the personal spiritual development of students as they study the deep truths of scripture, theology, and church practice, we foster the ongoing disconnect between information and application of truth to life. One of the key reasons for disillusionment among Christian leaders as they move through years of ministry is the tension between what they know and teach and what they actually experience in their individual walks with God. If we intend to stop this cycle, it must start in the seminary. Educational leaders must find ways to create a climate where spiritual direction is built into the fabric of the learning environment.

Christian leaders on all levels now realize that "business as usual" is not working—deep down inside something is missing. This sacred thirst is the beginning of a deeper intimacy with God. They are ready to shed old ways of being and explore new pathways of renewal that will form the soul. As I have already stated, the time has come to assess the realities of ministry and take the journey toward spiritual wellness. We need presidents and executive leaders of denominations, Christian organizations, and colleges who are committed to championing the ministry of spiritual direction toward this end. *If we believe that our highest calling is to prepare people to lead like Christ, it is imperative that relational spiritual formation must be at the core of our ministry culture.*

SPIRITUAL DIRECTION
RECOMMENDED READING

The books listed below are directly related to *spiritual direction* and are offered for those who desire to do further research in this field of study:

Alice Fryling, *Seeking God Together: An Introduction to Group Spiritual Direction* (Downers Grove, IL: InterVarsity Press, 2009)

Bruce Demarest, *Soulguide: Following Jesus as Spiritual Director* (Colorado Springs, CO: NavPress, 2003)

Carolyn Gratton, *Guidelines for Spiritual Direction* (Denville, NJ: Dimension Books, 1980)

David Benner, *Sacred Companions: The Gift of Spiritual Friendship & Direction* (Downers Grove, IL: InterVaristy Press, 2002)

David L. Fleming, *Draw Me into Your Friendship: A Literal Translation and a Contemporary Reading of the Spiritual Exercises* (St. Louis, MO: Institute of Jesuit Sourced, 1996)

Eugene H. Peterson, *Working the Angles: The Shape of Pastoral Integrity* (Grand Rapids, MI: William B. Eerdmans, 1987)

Francis de Sales, Jane de Chantal, *Letters of Spiritual Direction* (Mahwah, NJ: Paulist Press, 1988)

Francois Fenelon, *Spiritual Letters of Fenelon* (Hudson, NY: Idlewild Press, 1945)

Francis Kelly Nemeck and Marie Theresa Coombs, *The Way of Spiritual Direction* (Collegeville, MN: Liturgical Press, 1985)

Gary W. Moon and David G. Benner, eds., *Spiritual Direction and the Care of Souls* (Downers Grove, IL: InterVarsity Press, 2004)

Gerald G. May, *Care of Mind/Care of Spirit* (San Francisco: Harper and Row, 1982)

Henri Nouwen, *Spiritual Direction: Wisdom for the Long Walk of Faith* (New York: Estate of Henri J. M. Nouwen, 2006)

Jeannette A. Bakke, *Holy Invitations* (Grand Rapids, MI: Baker Books, 2000)

Janet K. Ruffing, *Spiritual Direction: Beyond the Beginnings* (Mahwah, NJ: Paulist Press, 2000)

Jean Laplace, *Preparing for Spiritual Direction* (Chicago: Franciscan Herald Press, 1988)

Margaret Guenther, *Holy Listening: The Art of Spiritual Direction* (Cambridge, MA: Cowley Publications, 1992)

Martin Thornton, *Spiritual Direction* (Eugene, OR: Wipf & Stock Publishers, 2012)

Maureen Conroy, *The Discerning Heart: Discovering a Personal God* (Chicago, IL: Loyola University Press, 1995)

Maureen Conroy, *Looking into the Well* (Chicago, IL: Loyola University Press, 1995)

Rose Mary Dougherty, *Group Spiritual Direction: Community for Discernment* (Mahwah, NJ: Paulist Press, 1985)

Susan Phillips, *Candlelight: Illuminating the Art of Spiritual Direction* (Nashville, TN: Abingdon Press, 2008)

Tad Dunne, *Spiritual Mentoring: Guiding People through Spiritual Exercises to Life Decisions* (New York: HarperSan Francisco, 1991)

Tilden Edwards, *Spiritual Director, Spiritual Companion* (Mahwah, NJ: Paulist Press, 2001)

William A. Barry and William J. Connolly, *The Practice of Spiritual Direction* (New York: HarperSanFrancisco, 1973)

William A. Barry, *Spiritual Direction and the Encounter with God: A Theological Inquiry* (New York: Paulist Press, 1992)

Endnotes

Chapter 1

[1] Richard Rohr, "Don't Miss The Second Half," U.S. Catholic, accessed May 24, 2013, http://www.uscatholic.org/2008/06/dont-miss-second-half

[2] Ruth Barton, "Spiritual Direction with Pastoral and Corporate Leaders," The Transforming Center, accessed August 3, 2013, http://www.transformingcenter.org/2013/04/spiritual-direction-with-pastoral-and-corporate-leaders/

[3] Kenneth Leech, *Soul Friend: Spiritual Direction in the Modern World* (Harrisburg, PA: Morehouse Publishing, 2001), xix.

Chapter 2

[1] As quoted in Dean R. Hoge and Jacqueline E. Wenger, *Pastors in Transition: Why Clergy Leave Local Church Ministry* (Grand Rapids, MI: William B. Eerdmans, 2005), 38.

[2] Fred Lehr, *Clergy Burnout* (Minneapolis, MN: Fortress Press, 2006), 4.

[3] Robert A. Johnson, *Owning Your Own Shadow: Understanding the Dark Side of the Psyche* (New York: Harper Collins, 1991), 4.

[4] Robert Mulholland, *The Deeper Journey: The Spirituality of Discovering Your True Self* (Downers Grove, IL: InterVarsity Press, 2006), 31.

[5] Patricia D. Brown, *Learning to Lead from Your Spiritual Center* (Nashville, TN: Abingdon, 1996), 11.

[6] Roy M. Oswald, *Clergy Self-Care: Finding Balance for Effective Ministry* (Herndon, VA: Alban Institute Publication, 1991), 10.

[7] Ibid., 102.

[8] Eugene H. Peterson, *Working the Angles: The Shape of Pastoral Integrity* (Grand Rapids, MI: William B. Eerdmans, 1987), 114.

[9] Ibid., 17.

Chapter 3

[1] Eugene Peterson, "The Inglorious Work of Spiritual Direction," *Leadership Journal*, accessed January, 1986, http://www.ctlibrary.com/search.html

[2] William A. Barry and William J. Connolly, *The Practice of Spiritual Direction* (New York: HarperSanFrancisco, 1973), 8.

[3] Henri Nouwen, *Spiritual Direction: Wisdom for the Long Walk of Faith* (New York: HarperSanFrancisco, 2006), ix.

[4] Kenneth Leech, *Soul Friend: The Practice of Spiritual Direction* (New York: Harper and Row, 1977), vii.

[5] Fara Impasato, "An Introduction to Spiritual Direction for Christian Counselors: Its Meaning, History, and Present Practice in the Roman Catholic Church," *Didaskalia* 8, no. 1 (1996): 29–30.

[6] Timothy Jones, *The Friendship Connection* (Wheaton, IL: Tyndale House Publishers, 1993), 7.

[7] Gerald G. May, *Care of Mind/Care of Spirit* (San Francisco: Harper and Row, 1982), 1.

[8] John O'Donohue, *Anam Cara: A Book of Celtic Wisdom* (New York: HarperCollins, 1997), xviii.

[9] Jerome M. Neufelder and Mary C. Coelho, eds., *Writings on Spiritual Direction by Great Christian Masters* (Minneapolis: Seabury Press, 1982), 36.

[10] Jones, *The Friendship Connection*, 17.

[11] Ibid., 8.

[12] Bruce Demarest, *Soulguide: Following Jesus as Spiritual Director* (Colorado Springs, CO: NavPress, 2003), 47.

[13] Roy M. Oswald, *How to Build a Support System for Your Ministry* (Herndon, VA: Alban Institute, 1991), 104.

[14] May, *Care of Mind/Care of Spirit*, 4.

[15] Ibid., 2.

[16] Forster Freeman, *Readiness for Ministry through Spiritual Direction* (Herndon, VA: Alban Institute, 1986), 6.

[17] James M. Houston, "The Independence Myth," *Christianity Today* 34, no. 1 (1990): 31.

[18] Impasato: 31.

[19] Lauren F. Winner, "From Mass Evangelist to Soul Friend," in *Christianity Today* 44, no. 11 (2000): 56.

[20] As quoted in Jennifer H. Disney, "Making Space for God," *Christianity Today* 45, no. 6 (2001): 88.

[21] Leech, *Soul Friend*, vi.

Chapter 4

[1] Gary W. Moon and David G. Benner, eds., *Spiritual Direction and the Care of Souls* (Downers Grove, IL: InterVarsity Press, 2004), 57.

[2] Lawrence J. Crabb, "The Passion/Wisdom Model of Spiritual Direction" (New Way Ministries, 2002), 20.

[3] Ibid.

[4] Darrell W. Johnson, *Experiencing the Trinity* (Vancouver, BC: Regent College Publishing 2002), 37.

[5] C. Baxter Kruger, *The Great Dance: The Christian Vision Revisited* (Vancouver, BC: Regent College Publishing, 2000), 24.

[6] William A. Barry, *Spiritual Direction and the Encounter with God: A Theological Inquiry* (New York: Paulist Press, 1992), 92.

[7] Ibid., 104.

[8] Ibid., 91.

[9] Ibid., 79–80.

[10] Margaret Guenther, *Holy Listening: The Art of Spiritual Direction* (Cambridge, MA: Cowley Publications, 1992), 46.

[11] Carolyn Gratton, *Guidelines for Spiritual Direction* (Denville, NJ: Dimension Books, 1980), 27.

[12] Bruce Demarest, *Soulguide: Following Jesus as Spiritual Director* (Colorado Springs, CO: NavPress, 2003), 140–141.

[13] Gratton, *Guidelines for Spiritual Direction*, 190–191.

[14] Moon and Benner, eds., *Spiritual Direction and the Care of Souls*, 34.

[15] As quoted in George A. Aschenbrenner, *Stretched for Greater Glory* (Chicago: Loyola Press, 2004), 84.

[16] John Ortberg, *The Life You've Always Wanted* (Grand Rapids, MI: Zondervan, 1997), 23.

[17] William Reiser, *Seeking God in All Things* (Collegeville, MN: Liturgical Press, 2004), 3.

[18] Francis W. Vanderwall, *Spiritual Direction: An Invitation to Abundant Life* (Ramsey, NJ: Paulist Press, 1981), 14.

[19] Maureen Conroy, *Looking into the Well: Supervision of*

Spiritual Directors (Chicago: Loyola University Press, 1995), 4.

[20] Thomas Green, *The Friend of the Bridegroom: Spiritual Direction and the Encounter with Christ* (Notre Dame, IN: Ave Maria Press, 2000), 33.

[21] Paul uses "to know" 50 times and John uses it 82 times. (See 1 Corinthians 2:16; 2 Corinthians 5:16; Ephesians 3:19; Philippians 3:10; 1 John 2:3; 3:14; 5:20.)

[22] Thoralf Gilbrant, ed., *The Complete Biblical Library: Greek-English Dictionary*, 16 vols., vol. 1 (Springfield, MO: The Complete Biblical Library, 1990), 623–626.

Chapter 5

[1] Maureen Conroy, *The Discerning Heart: Discovering a Personal God* (Chicago: Loyola University Press, 1993), xiii.

[2] Philip Sheldrake, *Traditions of Spiritual Guidance*, ed. Lavinia Byrne (Collegeville, MN: The Liturgical Press, 1990), 100.

[3] Philip Sheldrake, ed., *The Way of Ignatius Loyola: Contemporary Approaches to the Spiritual Exercises* (St. Louis, MO: The Institute of Jesuit Sources, 1991), 1.

[4] John Patrick Donnelly, *Ignatius of Loyola* (New York: Longman, 2004), xiii.

[5] Paul Doncoeur, *The Heart of Ignatius* (Baltimore, MD: Helicon Press, 1959), 19.

[6] Margaret Silf, *Companions of Christ: Ignatian Spirituality for Everyday Living* (Grand Rapids, MI: William B. Eerdmans Publishing, 2005), 9.

[7] Gilles Cusson, *Biblical Theology and the Spiritual Exercises* (St. Louis, MO: Institute of Jesuit Resources, 1998), 3.

[8] Karl Rahner, *Spiritual Exercises* (New York: Herder and

Herder, 1965), 52.

[9] Ibid., 16.

[10] Silf, *Companions of Christ*, 9–10.

[11] Rahner, *Spiritual Exercises*, 55–60.

[12] Donnelly, *Ignatius of Loyola*, 68.

[13] Jacqueline Syrup Bergan and Marie Schwan, *Praying with Ignatius of Loyola* (Winona, MN: Saint Mary's Press, 1991), 13.

[14] Margot Patterson, "Following in the Footsteps of Ignatius," *The National Catholic Reporter* (2001): 1.

Chapter 6

[1] St. Ignatius of Loyola, *The Spiritual Exercises of Saint Ignatius of Loyola*, trans. Anthony Mattola (New York: Doubleday, 1989), 47.

[2] John English, *Spiritual Freedom: From an Experience of the Ignatian Exercises to the Art of Spiritual Guidance.* 2nd ed. (Chicago: Loyola University Press, 1995), 20.

[3] A helpful tool in discerning the "false self" and the "inordinate attachments" that leaders need to address is the *Enneagram*. To learn more about this ancient work one can study Richard Rohr, *The Enneagram: A Christian Perspective* (New York: Crossroad Publishing Co., 2002). A valuable website is: www.enneagraminstitute.com

[4] David McQueen, Rev! Magazine's Bathroom Guide To Leadership (Loveland, CO: Group Publishing, 2007), 71.

[5] Dallas Willard, "Personal Soul Care," accessed March 26, 2012, http://www.dwillard.org/articles/artview.asp?artID=106

[6] Viktor E. Frankl, *Man's Search for Meaning* (New York: Simon & Schuster, 1985), 177.

[7] Leonard Cohen, "Anthem," *The Essential Leonard Cohen*, 2002, Sony BMG Music

[8] James F. Cobble, Jr. and Donald C. Houts, eds., *Well-Being in Ministry* (Matthews, NC: Christian Ministry Resources, 1999), 19–20.

Chapter 7

[1] Jules J. Toner, *A Commentary on St. Ignatius' Rules for the Discernment of Spirits* (St. Louis, MO: The Institute of Jesuit Sources), 39.

[2] Joseph A. Tetlow, *Ignatius Loyola Spiritual Exercises* (New York: Crossroad Publishing Company, 1992), 163.

[3] Toner, *A Commentary on St. Ignatius' Rules*, 7.

[4] William A. Barry, *Letting God Come Close* (Chicago: Loyola Press, 2001), 119.

[5] Timothy M. Gallagher, *Spiritual Consolation: An Ignatian Guide for the Greater Discernment of Spirits* (New York: Crossroad, 2007), 16.

[6] Maureen Conroy, *The Discerning Heart: Discovering a Personal God* (Chicago: Loyola University Press), xiv.

[7] Ibid., xv.

[8] Conroy, *The Discerning Heart: Discovering a Personal God*, 13.

[9] Francis W. Vanderwall, *Spiritual Direction: An Invitation to Abundant Life* (Ramsey, NJ: Paulist Press, 1981), 5.

[10] Toner, *A Commentary on St. Ignatius' Rules*, 112.

[11] Ibid., 144.

[12] Sheldrake, ed., *The Way of Ignatius Loyola: Contemporary Approaches to the Spiritual Exercises* (St. Louis, MO: The Institute

of Jesuit Sources, 1991), 32.

[13] Dan Allender and Tremper Longman, *The Cry of the Soul: How Our Emotions Reveal Our Deepest Questions About God* (Colorado Springs, CO: NavPress, 1994), 15.

[14] Kathleen Fischer, "Working with the Emotions in Spiritual Direction: Seven Guiding Principles," *Presence: An International Journal of Spiritual Direction* 12, no. 3 (2006).

[15] Francis Kelly Nemeck and Marie Theresa Coombs, *The Way of Spiritual Direction* (Collegeville, MN: Liturgical Press, 1985), 66.

[16] Gerald R. Grosh, *Quest for Sanctity: Seven Passages to Growth in Faith* (Wilmington, DE: Michael Glazier, 1988), 92.

Chapter 8

[1] Gary Moon, "Spiritual Direction: Meaning, Purpose, and Implications for Mental Health Professionals," *Journal of Psychology and Theology* 30, no. 4 (2002): 265.

[2] A. W. Tozer, *The Pursuit of God* (Harrisburg, PA: Christian Publications, 1968), 13.

[3] Ibid., 13–14.

[4] As quoted in Gary W. Moon and David G. Benner, eds. *Spiritual Direction and the Care of Souls* (Downers Grove, IL: InterVarsity Press, 1992), 56.

[5] William Reiser, *Seeking God in All Things* (Collegeville, MN: Liturgical Press, 2004), 65.

[6] William A. Barry, *Spiritual Direction and the Encounter with God: A Theological Inquiry* (New York: Paulist Press, 1992), 35.

[7] Elisabeth-Paule Labat as quoted by Bob Benson, Sr. and Michael W. Benson, *Disciplines for the Inner Life* (Hendersonville,

TN: Deeper Life Press, 1989), 230.

[8] William A. Barry, *Letting God Come Close* (Chicago: Loyola Press, 2001), 181.

[9] Joseph A. Tetlow, *Ignatius Loyola Spiritual Exercises* (New York: Crossroad Publishing Company, 1992), 34.

[10] Brother Lawrence, *The Practice of the Presence of God* (New Kensington, PA: Whitaker House, 1982), 61.

[11] Jean-Pierre de Caussade, *Abandonment to Divine Providence*, trans. John Beevers (New York: Doubleday, 1975), 16.

[12] Ibid., 52.

[13] Thomas R. Kelly, *A Testament of Devotion* (New York: Harper Collins, 1941), 3.

[14] Moon and Benner, eds., *Spiritual Direction and the Care of Souls*, 13.

[15] William A. Barry and William J. Connolly, *The Practice of Spiritual Direction* (New York: HarperSanFrancisco, 1973), 46.

[16] Jean Laplace, *Preparing for Spiritual Direction* (Chicago: Franciscan Herald Press, 1988), 33.

[17] See Philip Yancey, *Finding God in Unexpected Places* (New York: Moorings Publishing, 1995). Yancey has learned to detect the movement of God in the everyday and unexpected. He helps us to recognize God's presence in overlooked and ordinary times and places.

[18] The concepts of kataphatic and apophatic are terms used to represent two different basic approaches to spirituality. In all religious traditions there is a way of viewing spirituality that emphasizes the importance of images, symbols, and sensations. This kind of spirituality is known as kataphatic. On the other hand, the apophatic way emphasizes the truth of God that lies behind or

beyond all sensory or intellectual representations.

[19] Marion Cowan and John C. Futrell, *Companions in Grace* (St. Louis, MO: The Institute of Jesuit Sources, 2000), 89.

[20] John E. Dister, ed., *Spiritual Exercises of St. Ignatius* (Eugene, OR: Wipf and Stock Publishers, 2003), 2.

[21] Tad Dunne, *Spiritual Mentoring: Guiding People through Spiritual Exercises to Life Decisions* (New York: HarperSanFrancisco, 1991), 137.

[22] Barry, *Spiritual Direction and the Encounter with God: A Theological Inquiry,* 35.

[23] Rose Mary Dougherty, *Group Spiritual Direction: Community for Discernment* (New York: Paulist Press, 1985), 81.

[24] George A. Aschenbrenner, *Stretched for Greater Glory* (Chicago: Loyola Press, 2004), 15.

[25] Dunne, *Spiritual Mentoring: Guiding People through Spiritual Exercises to Life Decisions*, 84.

[26] John Baillie, *A Diary of Private Prayer* (New York: Fireside, 1949), 27.

[27] St. Augustine as quoted in David G. Benner, *The Gift of Being Yourself* (Downers Grove, IL: InterVarsity Press, 2004), 20.

[28] Meister Eckhart as quoted in Peter Scazzero, *Emotionally Healthy Spirituality* (Nashville, TN: Integrity Publishers, 2006), 65.

[29] John Calvin, *Institutes of the Christian Religion, Volume 1* (Grand Rapids, MI: Eerdmans Publishing Company, 1957), 37.

[30] Parish of St. Ignatius of Loyola, "Ignatian Spirituality," accessed March 26, 2012, http://www.bc.edu/bc_org/prs/stign/ignatian_spirit.html

[31] Philip Sheldrake, *Befriending Our Desires* (Ottawa, ON: Novalis, 2001), 25.

[32] Janet K. Ruffing, *Spiritual Direction: Beyond the Beginnings* (Mahwah, NJ: Paulist Press, 2000), 10.

[33] As quoted in Barry, "Beyond Counseling: Spiritual Direction," *Journal of Pastoral Counseling*, no. 36, (2001): 43–44.

[34] Sheldrake, *Befriending Our Desires,* 64.

[35] Reiser, *Seeking God in All Things,* 55.

[36] Ibid.

[37] Aschenbrenner, *Stretched for Greater Glory,* 7–8.

[38] Wilfrid Stinissen, *The Gift of Spiritual Direction: On Guidance and Care for the Soul* (Liguori, MO, Liguori Publications, 1999), 61.

[39] Madeline Birmingham and William J. Connolly, *Witnessing to the Fire: Spiritual Direction and the Development of Directors* (Kansas City, MO: Sheed & Ward, 1994), 51.

[40] Janet K. Ruffing, *Spiritual Direction: Beyond the Beginnings,* 13.

[41] John Eldredge, *The Journey of Desire* (Nashville, TN: Thomas Nelson, 2000), 166–167.

[42] Marian Cowan and John Carroll Futrell, *The Spiritual Exercises of St. Ignatius of Loyola: A Handbook for Directors* (New York: Le Jacq Publishing, 1982), 13.

[43] Karl Rahner, *Spiritual Exercises* (New York: Herder and Herder, 1965), 25.

[44] David Fleming, *Draw Me Into Your Friendship: The Spiritual Exercises* (St. Louis, MO: The Institute of Jesuit Source, 1996), 26.

[45] Valerie Isenhower and Judith Todd quoting Maureen Conroy, *Living into the Answers: A Workbook for Personal Spiritual Discernment* (Nashville, TN: Upper Room, 2008), 64.

Chapter 9

[1] Janet K. Ruffing, *Spiritual Direction: Beyond the Beginnings* (Mahwah, NJ: Paulist Press, 2000), 57.

[2] Thomas H. Green, *The Friend of the Bridegroom: Spiritual Direction and the Encounter with Christ* (Notre Dame, IN: Ave Maria Press, 2000), 10.

[3] Francis Kelly Nemeck and Marie Theresa Coombs, *The Way of Spiritual Direction* (Collegeville, MN: Liturgical Press, 1985), 83.

[4] Jan Johnson, "Surprised by God," *Conversations: A Forum for Authentic Transformation* 5, no. 1 (Spring 2007): 26.

[5] David L. Fleming, *Draw Me Into Your Friendship* (St. Louis, MO: The Institute of Jesuit Sources, 1996), 14.

[6] Francis W. Vanderwall, *Spiritual Direction: An Invitation to Abundant Life* (Ramsey, NJ: Paulist Press, 1981), 87.

[7] Philip Sheldrake, ed., *The Way of Ignatius Loyola: Contemporary Approaches to the Spiritual Exercises* (St. Louis, MO: The Institute of Jesuit Sources, 1991), 179.

[8] Timothy Jones, *The Friendship Connection* (Wheaton, IL: Tyndale House Publishers, 1993), 37.

[9] Francis Kelly Nemeck and Marie Theresa Coombs, *The Way of Spiritual Direction*, 91.

[10] Gerald G. May, *Care of Mind/Care of Spirit* (San Francisco: Harper and Row, 1982), 116.

[11] Gary W. Moon and David G. Benner, eds., *Spiritual Direction and the Care of Souls* (Downers Grove, IL: InterVarsity Press, 2004), 57.

[12] Rose Mary Dougherty, *Group Spiritual Direction: Community for Discernment* (New York: Paulist Press, 1985), 2.

[13] Alice Fryling quoting Kenneth Blue, *Seeking God Together* (Downers Grove, IL: Intervarsity Press, 2009), 41.

[14] As quoted in Thomas N. Hart, *The Art of Christian Listening* (Ramsey, NJ: Paulist Press, 1980), 1.

[15] Thomas H. Green, *The Friend of the Bridegroom: Spiritual Direction and the Encounter with Christ*, 40.

[16] Margaret Guenther, *Holy Listening: The Art of Spiritual Direction* (Cambridge, MA: Cowley Publications, 1992), 65.

[17] Ibid., 65.

[18] Jean Laplace, *Preparing for Spiritual Direction* (Chicago, IL: Franciscan Herald Press, 1988), 106.

[19] Nemeck and Coombs, *The Way of Spiritual Direction*, 128.

[20] Ibid.

[21] Wilfrid Stinissen, *The Gift of Spiritual Direction: On Spiritual Guidance and Care for the Soul*, trans. Joseph B. Board (Liguori, MO: Liguori Publications, 1999), 50.

[22] A. W. Tozer, *The Knowledge of the Holy* (San Francisco: Harper and Row Publishers, 1961), 9.

[23] William A. Barry, *Letting God Come Close* (Chicago: Loyola Press, 2001), 23.

[24] Delcy Kuhlman, "Gifts of the Journey," *Conversations: A Forum for Authentic Transformation* 5, no. 1 (Spring 2007): 50.

[25] William A. Barry, *Spiritual Direction and the Encounter with God: A Theological Inquiry* (New York: Paulist Press, 1992), 62.

[26] Katherine Marie Dyckman and L. Patrick Carroll, *Inviting the Mystic: Supporting the Prophet* (New York: Paulist Press, 1981), 55.

[27] Gerald R. Grosh, *Quest for Sanctity: Seven Passages to Growth in Faith* (Wilmington, DE: Michael Glazier, 1988), 91.

[28] Joseph A. Tetlow, *Ignatius Loyola Spiritual Exercises* (New York: Crossroad Publishing Company, 1992), 58.

[29] Tilden Edwards, *Spiritual Director, Spiritual Companion* (Mahwah, NJ: Paulist Press, 2001), 24.

[30] Len Sperry, "Integrating Spiritual Direction Functions in the Practice of Psychotherapy," *Journal of Psychology and Theology* 31, no. 1 (2003): 4.

[31] Frank J. Houdek, *Guided by the Spirit: A Jesuit Perspective on Spiritual Direction* (Chicago: Loyola Press, 1996), 9-10.

[32] Marian Cowan and John Carroll Futrell, *The Spiritual Exercises of St. Ignatius of Loyola: A Handbook for Directors* (New York: Le Jacq Publishing, 1982), 15.

[33] Dyckman and Carroll, *Inviting the Mystic: Supporting the Prophet*, 62.

[34] Houdek, *Guided by the Spirit: A Jesuit Perspective on Spiritual Direction,* 90.

[35] William A. Barry and William J. Connolly, *The Practice of Spiritual Direction*, 51.

[36] Ibid., 70–71.

[37] Kenneth Leech, *Soul Friend: The Practice of Spiritual Direction* (New York: Harper and Row, 1977), iv.

Chapter 10

[1] Wilfrid Stinissen, *The Gift of Spiritual Direction: On Spiritual Guidance and Care for the Soul*, trans. Joseph B. Board (Liguori, MO: Liguori Publications, 1999), 17.

[2] Thomas H. Green, *The Friend of the Bridegroom: Spiritual Direction and the Encounter with Christ* (Notre Dame, IN: Ave

Maria Press, 2000), 63.

[3] Jerome M. Neufelder and Mary C. Coelho, eds., *Writings on Spiritual Direction by Great Christian Masters* (Minneapolis, MN: Seabury Press, 1982), 24.

[4] Stinissen, *The Gift of Spiritual Direction: On Spiritual Guidance and Care for the Soul*, 4–5.

[5] Neufelder and Coelho, eds., *Writings on Spiritual Direction by Great Christian Masters*, 37.

[6] Eugene Peterson, "The Inglorious Work of Spiritual Direction," *Leadership Journal*, accessed May 19, 2004, http://www.ctlibrary.com/search.html

[7] Francis Kelly Nemeck and Marie Theresa Coombs, *The Way of Spiritual Direction* (Collegeville, MN: Liturgical Press, 1985), 71.

[8] James Houston, *The Transforming Friendship* (Oxford, England: Lion Publishing, 1989), 283–284.

[9] Kevin T. Barry, "Beyond Counseling: Spiritual Direction," *Journal of Pastoral Counseling* 36 (2001): 45.

[10] Alice Fryling, *Seeking God Together: An Introduction to Group Spiritual Direction* (Downers Grove, IL: InterVarsity Press, 2009), 26.

[11] Adapted from Alice Fryling, *Seeking God Together, An Introduction to Group Spiritual Direction*.

[12] Roy M. Oswald, *Clergy Self-Care: Finding Balance for Effective Ministry* (Herndon, VA: Alban Institute Publication, 1991), 12.

[13] David G. Benner, "Nurturing Spiritual Growth," *Journal of Psychology and Theology* 30, no.4 (2002): 360.

Appendix

[1] Gerald G. May, *Care of Mind/Care of Spirit* (San Francisco: Harper and Row, 1982), 4.

[2] As quoted in Jerome M. Neufelder and Mary C. Coelho, eds., *Writings on Spiritual Direction by Great Christian Masters* (Minneapolis, MN: Seabury Press, 1982), 40.

[3] Stephen A. Macchia, "Spiritual Formation and the Pastor: A Vision for Shortening the Distance between Pew and Pulpit," *Conversations: A Forum for Authentic Transformation* 5, no. 1 (Spring 2007): 38.

[4] Forster Freeman, "Spiritual Direction for Seminarians," *Theological Education* 24, no. 1 (Autumn 1987): 40.

[5] Ibid., 48.

Made in the USA
San Bernardino, CA
24 March 2016